tre

Lea and
Teach g with ICT

Also available

Unlocking Creativity
Teaching Across the Curriculum
Edited by Robert Fisher and Mary Williams
1-84312-092-5

Unlocking Literacy 2e
Edited by Robert Fisher and Mary Williams
1-84312-386-X

Unlocking Speaking and Listening
Edited by Pamela Hodson and Deborah Jones
1-84312-392-4

Unlocking Learning and Teaching with ICT

Identifying and Overcoming Barriers

Helena Gillespie

 David Fulton Publishers

This edition reprinted 2007 by Routledge
2 Park Square, Milton Park, Abingdon, Oxon, OX14 4RN
Simultaneously published in the USA and Canada
By Routledge
270 Madison Avenue, New York, NY 10016

First published in Great Britain in 2006 by David Fulton Publishers

10 9 8 7 6 5 4 3 2

British Library Cataloguing in Publication Data
A catalogue record for this book is available from the British Library.

ISBN: 1 84312 376 2

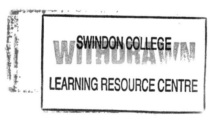
Typeset by FiSH Books, Enfield, Middx.
Printed and bound in Great Britain.

Contents

Acknowledgements

This is the first book I have written on my own and writing it has been enjoyable, thought-provoking and at times downright difficult. I owe a great deal of thanks to Tracey Alcock and the team at David Fulton Publishers for their help and encouragement. I would also like to thank all my colleagues and students, past and present at UEA, who have been both inspirational and supportive since I first entered teacher education four years ago.

There are many people who have helped with the book in practical ways, not least Zoë Morgan whose help with proof reading and indexing was much appreciated.

The ideas which gave rise to this book came form the many teachers and children I have worked with in the past, and I'm fortunate to still know lots of teachers who, while I was writing this book, kept me well supplied with information about real life in their classrooms. For tolerating my quizzing them in detail and for being willing to put their experiences into words I'd like to extend my thanks all the teachers I know, especially Eileen Stephens, Clare Cox, Gill Barrett and the 'old girls and boys' of the College of St Paul's and St Mary's, Cheltenham.

Finally I need to thank my family, especially my Mum Pauline, for making me believe I could write a book, and my husband, Rob, without whose patience, encouragement and willingness to cook the dinner and do the washing up, this book would never have been finished.

Helena Gillespie

Introduction: Learning with technology

Computers are useless. They can only give you answers.

(Pablo Picasso)

For those who have, like me, spent many hours staring at a computer screen trying to find some answer or another, Picasso's famous quote is perplexing. If only computers really could just give us the answers. Unfortunately, finding the *right* answers is more difficult than it sometimes appears. To do that, we must also make sure we are asking the right questions.

A story which has become very popular in our computer-dominated generation is Douglas Adams' *The Hitchhiker's Guide to the Galaxy*. In this cautionary tale, the people of earth build a huge computer to find out the 'ultimate answer to the ultimate question'. The answer, it turns out, is 42, but unfortunately no one was really sure what the question was in the first place. This story strikes a chord because for the past 15 years in education, I have met many people who have been trying to find 'answers' to complex educational issues by using computers in teaching and learning. Computers have been used to address issues like assessment, motivation and meeting individual needs. Computers have been promising to solve a great many problems and to answer important questions. However, I believe to a large extent these issues remain unresolved and the questions unanswered.

I have always tried to maintain a positive attitude to Information and Communications Technology (ICT) in teaching and learning. At the root of this lay personal interest in and enthusiasm for computers, and a developing understanding of how they can transform education for the better. Occasionally, during my time as a teacher and learner, I have seen ICT make a real difference: a moment of revelation when a programmer made a simple piece of code work; when a boy read fluently from the screen in a way he never did from a book; when a child created a beautiful picture; when teachers smile at photos taken during a school visit. Yet these moments, where computers really did seem to find the 'answers' for teachers and learners, are few and far between. Despite extensive studies by academics and governments (Harrison, Comber, *et al.* 2002; DfES 2003a; DfES 2003b), ICT is still to prove its worth. There is evidence to suggest that using computers in teaching can be motivational, but there is still very little evidence to suggest it is having a significant impact on pupil attainment in any subject and at any level. Considering the amount of money, time and effort invested in ICT, this lack of evidence of improvement in attainment seems – to put it mildly – a little disappointing.

My positive attitude to ICT is tempered by pragmatism about the current situation. It seems highly unlikely that having invested so heavily, policy is going to change, and the role of ICT in teaching and learning in schools in general is going to diminish. The future policy calls for ICT to work towards 'Fulfilling the Potential', where the possible contribution of ICT to future developments in teaching and learning is outlined optimistically:

> Information and communications technology (ICT) and e-learning have a massive contribution to make to all aspects of this reform agenda. For example:
>
> - ICT can make a significant contribution to teaching and learning across all subjects and ages, inside and outside the curriculum.
> - ICT can provide opportunities to engage and motivate children and young people and meet their individual learning needs.
> - ICT can help link school and home by providing access to teaching and learning materials, and to assessment and attendance data, from home.
> - ICT can enable schools to share information and good practice in networked learning communities.
> - Intelligent information management systems within schools can support school leadership.
> - Integrated curriculum and management information systems can help schools monitor individual pupils' progress for assessment for learning as well as for administrative purposes.
> - Use of shared drives in schools to bank lesson plans and other resources can produce vast savings in time and effort for teachers.
>
> (DfES 2003a)

It is this optimistic vision from the policy-makers and my own personal enthusiasm for ICT which have inspired me to write this book. Because, fervour and forward-looking policy aside, there is still a huge gap between what is it is possible to achieve by using ICT in teaching and learning, and what is actually being achieved.

The minefield of ICT

Embarking on writing a book about ICT is a minefield of controversy, not least because it means raising controversial issues. Discussing these, even in detail, seems unlikely to make them less controversial. So rather than duck the controversy, it seems more productive to meet it head on. To this end some of the issues might be:

- What do we mean by teaching and learning?
- What do we mean by ICT?
- What do we mean by barriers?

What do we mean by teaching and learning?

The Oxford English Dictionary describes the verb 'to teach' as *to enable or induce by instruction or training*, and 'to learn' as *to get knowledge, skill or ability by study, experience or being taught.*

In practice, the arts of teaching and learning are substantially more complex than these simple definitions. Teaching and learning are both defined by a complex human relationship, by communication which is both verbal and non-verbal, and mood, attitude and personality. To teach and learn effectively there needs to be clear communication between those involved. Crucially, when teaching and learning is at its best it involves a two-way process, with all participants both teaching and learning.

What do we mean by ICT?

Information and Communications Technology is a term which covers a range of hardware (machines) and software (applications of the machines). In schools now it might mean any of the following:

- personal computers;
- Apple Macintosh computers;
- digital cameras and digital video cameras;
- image scanners;
- printers and faxes;
- handheld computers;
- datalogging equipment;
- calculators;
- programmable robots.

These could support learning in ways such as:

- word processing;
- data collection and handling;
- image creation and manipulation;
- music creation and editing;
- communication via electronic mail, electronic discussion and electronic chat;
- research using CD-ROMs or the Internet;
- controlling movement.

ICT in schools can mean all of the above and more, and the parameters of the subject are expanding all the time. As technology becomes increasingly miniaturised, devices are becoming ever more portable, so it is now possible to make a handheld computer – which can connect to the Internet – deal with email, word process and act as an electronic diary. All of this in a device which is substantially smaller than the first mobile phones made back in the 1980s. Distinctions between devices are increasingly blurred, and these handheld computers can now perform many of the functions of modern mobile phones as well as laptop PCs, and new generation phones can access the Internet, take photographs and play music. It seems likely that in a few short years, these devices will merge, and that each of us will own just one device for work, for communication and for leisure.

In the educational community, although most schools still have the some of the 'grey box' generation of computers remaining, the future is one where these multimedia devices will play a full role in pupils' education. To adapt teaching and learning to harness fully the potential of the available technology is one of the greatest challenges which face schools in the future.

What do we mean by barriers?

Simply put, barriers prevent something from happening. In this context, the barriers are the things which prevent teachers from utilising the full potential of ICT in teaching and learning. In a recent review of research carried out by BECTA (The British Educational Communications Technology Association), a wide range of barriers to using ICT in teaching are identified. They fall into four categories: resource-related factors, factors associated with training, knowledge and skills, attitudinal and personality factors and institutional and cultural factors (BECTA 2003d). These factors are organised into two levels: into the first level fall those concerned with the teacher themselves, and in the second level are those concerned with the school or institution.

Teacher-level barriers

- lack of time – for both formal training and self-directed exploration and for preparing ICT resources for lessons;
- lack of self-confidence in using ICT;
- negative experiences with ICT in the past;
- fear of embarrassment in front of pupils and colleagues, loss of status and an effective degrading of professional skills;
- classroom management difficulties when using ICT, especially where pupil-to-computer ratios are poor;
- lack of the knowledge necessary to enable teachers to resolve technical problems when they occur;
- lack of personal change management skills;
- perception that technology does not enhance learning;
- lack of motivation to change long-standing pedagogical practices;
- perception of computers as complicated and difficult to use.

School-level barriers

- lack of ICT equipment and the cost of acquiring, using and maintaining ICT resources;
- lack of access to ICT equipment due to organisational factors such as the deployment of computers in ICT suites rather than classrooms;
- obsolescence of software and hardware;
- unreliability of equipment;
- lack of technical support;
- lack of administrative support;
- lack of institutional support through leadership, planning and the involvement of teachers as well as managers in implementing change;
- lack of training differentiated according to teachers' existing ICT skill levels;
- lack of training focusing on integrating technology in the classroom rather than simply teaching basic skills.

(BECTA 2003d, p. 2)

These factors, based mostly on small-scale research projects done in the USA, have much in common with the barriers identified in this book. There are some projects included in the review which are UK-based, but most of these are concerned with barriers encountered by teachers in, or just after, training. It is unsurprising that research done in the USA on this topic is raising these issues, which closely relate to the issues raised by this book, which are in turn largely UK-research based. There are many common factors within teaching and learning with ICT, in all contexts, UK, USA, in primary schools, in the secondary phase, with new teachers and with experienced teachers. For that reason this book is organised thematically, around the nature of barriers rather than phases or subjects.

Identifying and overcoming barriers – using this book

Teachers are driven to do what is best for their pupils by the strong vocation that keeps them all in the job, despite the many trials and tribulations of the average working day in a school. Generally speaking, teachers will do what is best for their pupils, whatever it takes. If we are to persuade teachers to make the changes to teaching and learning which are required to make the vision for ICT a reality, they must be convinced that the changes are in the best interests of their pupils. In short, it must be demonstrated that ICT is worth the effort – that it will help pupils achieve more, that it will foster inclusion and improve levels of engagement, that it will free teachers to engage more closely with their pupils and that it will help produce pupils who are well-equipped to make the world a better place when they leave school.

In order to harness this strong vocation, and help teachers and schools make full use of the potential of ICT, it is necessary to identify what is currently preventing the potential being reached. Identifying those barriers, examining them and then suggesting ways to overcome them is the purpose of this book. Teachers at all stages of their career, from the first steps in Initial Teacher Training, through induction and into continuing professional development, may encounter some of these barriers in making ICT successful in teaching and learning. This book is also aimed at school managers and policy-makers who may encounter these barriers. The book is also intended to support further study and research into ICT and learning, and refers to a wide range of websites, reports and publications.

The first stage of identifying and overcoming the barriers is to consider current policy and practice. Schools and teachers need to develop an idea of the wider context of their own practice, and Chapter 1 is designed to enable them to do this.

Chapters 2 to 6 examine the barriers in particular areas. These sections have a common format:

- Background and introduction
- Definition of terms
- Case studies and literature reviews
- Issues raised
- Barriers summarised

- Overcoming the barriers and identifying benefits
- Further reading and references.

This common chapter structure will help readers utilise the book in different ways; for example, those looking for an overview of learning technology in schools could read the first sections of each chapter. Those engaged in teaching and seeking definitions of some of the specific vocabulary might use the definition of terms section. Those researching and looking for useful case studies might read the case study/literature review section. Those looking for practical help might read about overcoming barriers and identifying benefits. Although each chapter deals with particular issues, links are made between each one. Finally, Chapter 7 will examine practical approaches to action planning, giving practical advice on how to approach identifying and overcoming the barriers. In conclusion, the final chapter seeks to look ahead to the future of learning technology and is positive about the benefits that can be gained in teaching and learning once the barriers are removed.

References

BECTA (2003d) *What the Research Says About Barriers to the Use of ICT in Teaching*, BECTA, Coventry.

DfES (2003a) *Fulfilling the Potential: Transforming Teaching and Learning Through ICT in Schools*. DfES, London.

DfES (2003b) *The big pICTure: The Impact of ICT on Attainment, Motivation and Learning*. DfES, London.

Harrison, C., Comber, C., Fisher, T., Haw, K., Lewin, C., Luzner, E., McFarlane, A., Mavers, D., Scrimshaw, P., Somekh, B., Watling, R. (2002) *ImpaCT2: The Impact of Information and Communication on Pupil Learning and Attainment. Strand 1 Report*. DfES, London.

Mavers, D., Scrimshaw, P., Somekh, B., Watling, R. (2002) *ImpaCT2: The Impact of Information and Communication on Pupil Learning and Attainment. Strand 1 Report*. DfES, London.

CHAPTER 1

Information technology in schools: policy and practice

Introduction

The world of education and schools is changing rapidly. This is due in no small part to the fact that learning technology is ever-evolving. Some teachers and educators hold polarised views on this evolution and change in our classrooms: at one end of the scale there are those who believe education cannot face the future without learning technology being the very root of what schools do; and at the other end are those who think that learning technology has nothing to offer the education of young people. Most teachers I have met place themselves at neither of these poles, but are somewhere in the middle. Many remain sceptical about whether learning technology can or should contribute significantly to education, others feel that there are many potential benefits. However what nearly every teacher I know has in common on this issue is that they would like to know more in order to come to a real judgement about what effect computers can have in their classrooms.

The majority of teachers and those involved in education feel that 'the jury is still out' on whether learning technology is a crucial element of education for the twenty-first century. In a recent large-scale study into the impact of ICT on teaching and learning (DfES 2003b), general findings indicated a positive relationship between pupils' attainment and use of ICT in most subjects and in most phases. In the meantime the message we are receiving from commerce and industry is that we must more effectively prepare children for the world of work. Along with literacy and numeracy, skills in using Information Technology (perhaps more appropriately known as Information and Communication Technology in many schools) are seen as central to being effectively prepared. This seems like a good reason itself to include ICT in the work of education. But I believe there are also reasons to include it that are nothing to do with learning skills for later life. I believe there are some things which can be done with ICT which are better, easier and more useful than if they are done in traditional ways. In short, I believe ICT has an intrinsic value in education.

We are not yet at a stage with ICT development in schools where we are making the best use of this resource. Studies such as 'The big pICTure' (DfES 2003b) have demonstrated a link between enhanced pupil achievement and ICT, but this and other studies such as ImpaCT 2 (Harrison, Comber, *et al.* 2002) have struggled to show the significance of this link. This chapter discusses the current state of learning technology in schools, looking at each key stage in turn and examining the issues in ICT in education.

Aims of this chapter

The aim of this chapter is to outline some of the current issues in Information and Communications Technology in schools. This is done through six 'sketches taken in the classroom'. These sketches are, of course, fictitious, but the situations they portray reflect the current practice in many schools, and highlight the problems, benefits and issues which teachers from foundation stage to key stage 5 face in the early twenty-first century. Each sketch does not represent the full range of issues which occur in each setting, but a snapshot of a particular situation.

From each sketch, issues relating to curriculum, assessment, content and training are discussed. This is not to imply that the issues raised in each section are exclusive to that key stage, in fact many of the issues are current across key stages. As any teacher knows, the range of issues which they face daily and weekly in schools seems to grow. These issues include:

- developing planning procedures;
- schemes of work;
- managing formative assessment;
- summative assessment and its implications, both internal and external to the school;
- pupils with special educational needs;
- pupils who are gifted and talented;
- pupils who have English as an additional language;
- inclusion;
- addressing varied modes of learning;
- managing time and resources;
- managing professional development.

All these issues to some extent impact on how ICT can be used in teaching and learning, yet teachers who have effective teaching strategies tend to make good use of ICT as well. In its turn the practice of a confident teacher breeds a willingness to experiment with new teaching approaches, which can lead to further success.

A pervasive theme of this chapter is change, and all teachers, wherever they teach, will recognise that things are changing rapidly in education. Changes in technology occur even faster, and many have long since abandoned trying to make good use their own teaching of every new resource as it is launched. This seems a sensible approach. Rather teachers need to recognise the changes in their field and plan for and manage their introduction into their overall approach. Each of the teachers described in the sketches below is making use of ICT effectively in their teaching, yet there is much more that each teacher can do.

Policy in ICT

There are few areas of educational policy more contentious than ICT. This may be because ICT has been the focus of substantial financial investment since the beginning of the NGfL project in 1998, and many schools and teachers remain to be convinced that ICT is providing value for money in terms of improved pupil achievement. Issues of funding are explored more fully in Chapter 2.

Several studies have been the basis for current policy in ICT. In 2002, the extensive *ImpaCT2* study (Harrison, Comber, *et al.* 2002) looked at three strands of ICT in education:

- the impact of ICT on pupil learning and achievement;
- the perception of ICT in home, school and community;
- learning at home and school.

Drawing on both original and existing research, the study provides a basis for ICT policy-making in the twenty-first century. It was funded by the DfES and carried out by BECTA (The British Educational Communications Technology Association) who, although independent of the education department, provide a good deal of data and advice to the DfES on ICT. In addition there are organisations like Nesta Futurelab who fund and support small-scale research and literature reviews into innovation in ICT.

The fundamentals of government policy in ICT are set out in *Fulfilling the Potential* (DfES 2003a) where the ICT agenda is closely linked to other education reform issues, such as workforce reform and curriculum development. This policy statement is intended to lead schools towards becoming 'e-confident'. The paper sets out likely trends in ICT provision in education from 2006 onwards in:

- connectivity
- networking
- computers
- managed learning environments
- whole-class displays
- creative technologies
- access technologies.

The paper also describes the 'next steps' needed to take schools forward in these areas. Despite being high on ideas, and to some extent, rhetoric, and low on practical suggestions, *Fulfilling the Potential* is likely to be the basis for future policy developments in ICT.

Information and Communication Technology in practice: Sketches taken in the classroom

The foundation stage

Ashbury Nursery is a busy and lively place. The nursery teacher, Gemma Barrett, encourages a learning environment where access to space and resources is open to all. She has a close working relationship with the two teaching assistants.

Gemma has integrated learning technology into her setting in a number of ways. In one corner there is a story tape, for the children to listen to using headphones. The children enjoy this way of hearing their favourite stories, and they know which buttons to press by remembering how traffic lights work. The 'stop' button has a red sticker, the play a green one and the pause button has a yellow sticker. The children enjoy using this tape recorder independently, and each morning Gemma changes the tape. Over in the reading corner, a small group of children are re-living last week's autumn walk, through a book made by the teaching assistant with digital photos, which the children took, with a little help. Enjoying the book with the group is a boy with communication difficulties, who is working with a teaching assistant to extend his vocabulary, prompted by the book.

There are two computers in the nursery. Each has a range of curriculum software including simple word processing packages, which enable children to use word-banks to write rather than the keyboard, a drawing package and some stories on CD. Today the children are working in pairs on a counting program. They are using a large 'rollerball mouse' and a concept keyboard to make the program work.

Considering this situation, what are the ICT issues?

The foundation stage curriculum and assessment

The foundation stage curriculum (DfEE and QCA 2000) includes an early learning goal for information and communications technology within the Knowledge and Understanding of the World area of learning. It emphasises that computers and other ICT devices can be used as tools to further children's knowledge and understanding of the world around them. They use ICT devices to gather information too, and where appropriate practitioners model the use of ICT in the setting to encourage children to develop independent skills. The stepping stones of the curriculum suggest that children move from showing an interest in ICT, through learning how to operate devices and finally to identifying the different uses of learning technology. This diversity and variety of use is evident in the foundation stage setting described above.

In addition, some of the fundamental principles of the foundation stage curriculum can relate to learning technology. Some practitioners wonder whether learning technology is of real use in the foundation stage. However, looking at some of the fundamental principles outlined on pages 11 and 12 of the foundation stage guidance (DfEE and QCA 2000), learning technology can be seen to have some real relevance to what the curriculum sees as the best practice for children at this early stage of their learning and development. See Table 1.1

Assessing learning in the early years is a challenge. Elsewhere in the primary phase, assessment is sometimes seen as synonymous with work produced on paper. In the foundation stage, such an approach is impractical and inappropriate in many areas of the curriculum. However, there are many uses of ICT which can support assessment. On a basic level, some computer programs record children's performance, but the really effective use of ICT in assessment in the foundation stage is the ability to record images, both still and moving, of what children do. In the setting described, the digital photos taken on the children's walk are both a reminder to the practitioners of what the children did and how they reacted on their autumn walk. The ability to easily, cheaply and quickly capture images has a great deal of potential.

Training for early years practitioners

In the setting described above, all the adults are able to use the ICT provision in their teaching. However in many settings, levels of practitioner confidence and competence in using ICT is variable. This is a result of previous training arrangements which did not serve these sorts of settings well. In some settings, one practitioner (not always the person with qualified teacher status) has led the development of ICT in the curriculum and where this has happened effective practice has been nurtured. However, until comprehensive and regular

Table 1.1 Foundation stage principles and ICT

Principles for early years education from the *Curriculum Guidance for the Foundation Stage*, pages 11 and 12	The role of ICT in supporting this principle
Effective education requires both a relevant curriculum and practitioners who understand and are able to implement the curriculum requirements. To be effective, an early years curriculum should be carefully structured. For children to have rich and stimulating experiences, the learning environment should be well planned and well organised. Above all, effective learning and development for young children requires high-quality care and education by practitioners.	ICT can support practitioners in developing effective planning and assessment strategies. The range of devices now available, including desktop and laptop computers, tablet PCs, robots and battery operated toys, still and moving digital cameras, tape and CD players and recorders, video and DVD players etc mean that ICT has a wide range of applications in the early years setting.
Effective education requires practitioners who understand that children develop rapidly during the early years – physically, intellectually, emotionally and socially.	ICT provides adaptable learning resources which can support children's learning through a range of stages of development.
Practitioners should ensure that all children feel included, secure and valued. No child should be excluded or disadvantaged.	ICT and the range of devices and tools it includes can be significant in promoting the inclusion of children with a range of emotional, cognitive and physical barriers to learning.
Early years experience should build on what children already know and can do. Parents and practitioners should work together.	Children come into settings with a wide variety of experiences of using technology, and a good range of ICT devices in the setting can build on knowledge and understanding gained at home or in other settings.
There should be opportunities for children to engage in activities planned by adults and also those that they plan or initiate themselves. Well-planned, purposeful activity and appropriate intervention by practitioners will engage children in the learning process.	Many ICT devices can be used by children independently, which allows children to initiate their own learning. In addition these devices can be used flexibly by practitioners in a range of activities.
Practitioners must be able to observe and respond appropriately to children.	ICT can be used to communicate in a variety of ways with children.
These principles are the basis on which every part of this guidance has been developed, and are reflected throughout.	ICT can be used and applied throughout the six areas of learning.

arrangements for professional development in all areas are put in place, it seems likely that some practitioners will continue to be under-skilled in this crucial area. A fuller examination of the issues relating to training teachers and other practitioners is in Chapter 4.

Connectivity, hardware and software

The issue of connectivity (connection of ICT devices to a network and ultimately the Internet) in the foundation stage is often disregarded. The reason given is that much of the content on the Internet is unsuitable for use in the foundation stage because of its dependence on text. However, there are many websites now being developed with content designed for the foundation stage. In addition, the advantages of being able to communicate using sound and pictures means there is much potential for further development in this area. Although opportunities to use the Internet in teaching and learning in the foundation stage at the time of writing are limited, the potential for development in this area is considerable.

There is a wide a variety of hardware and software available which can have an application in the foundation stage. There is a range of 'content' driven software available, mostly in the form of games and stories which develop basic reading and mathematical skills in the format of games and activities. Such software, however, is not the only use of PCs in the foundation stage. 'Content-free' software such as drawing programs are particularly exciting when used in conjunction with tablet PCs where the children can draw directly onto the screen with a stylus. A range of input devices in place of the 'traditional' keyboard and mouse arrangement give added accessibility to ICT software for all pupils, including those with some motor or visual impairment.

The range of non-computer-based ICT is widening and many devices are becoming increasingly robust and easy to operate. Digital cameras are a case in point, and there are many and varied uses of these in the foundation stage. In addition, the use of CDs for music and spoken word is increasing in settings where children's home experience means they are increasingly able to operate these devices independently. The range and scope of the foundation stage and the varied settings in which learning takes place means that the application of ICT in the early years is a quickly growing and developing area.

Key stage 1

Summer Lane Primary has one key stage 1 class, of mixed year 1 and 2 pupils. The teacher, Rob Gallagher, is an ICT enthusiast. He works hard to integrate ICT throughout the curriculum. In this week's plans, the children are going to use tape recorders in music, a video in history and in literacy they are using the set of laptops to work on writing using a word-bank program. This week's literacy objective relates to using appropriate descriptive words, and the children are using a grid in 'Clicker' to create their own descriptive sentences about an alien. Rob has created a number of grids to match the reading abilities of his pupils and each of the five groups in the class will have an opportunity to use the laptops once in the literacy session in the week.

Around the classroom the work on the walls shows where ICT has been used in art, to make patterns in various shades of green, and in maths where 'Logo' has been used to make simple shapes. In this way the children use a range of software in their learning, both with firm objectives and in open-ended activities.

Considering this situation, what are the ICT issues?

Key stage 1 curriculum and assessment, direct teaching and integration

The key stage 1 National Curriculum has a dual approach to ICT. It sets out the skills to be acquired and also states that ICT should be used as a teaching and learning tool in other curriculum areas. The requirements are set out in the introduction to the curriculum:

> Pupils should be given opportunities to apply and develop their ICT capability through the use of ICT tools to support their learning in all subjects. At key stage 1, there are no statutory requirements to teach the use of ICT in the programmes of study for the non-core foundation subjects. Teachers should use their judgement to decide where it is appropriate to teach the use of ICT across these subjects at key stage 1. At other key stages, there are statutory requirements to use ICT in all subjects, except physical education.
>
> (DfEE and QCA 1999)

This means that to make ICT effective at key stage 1, the teacher needs to directly teach ICT skills and design lessons which incorporate the use of ICT into the core subjects (English, Mathematics and Science) at least. This means that planning for the subject to be taught and incorporated needs to be at all levels: long, medium and short term. In addition, where ICT skills are assessed, it should be through its use in other subjects as well as in relation to the individual ICT skills. In Rob's key stage 1 classroom, ICT is successful because it is carefully planned into teaching, such as group work like literacy hour, and he has spent some time at the beginning of the school year enabling the children to organise themselves when using the computer, knowing what to touch (the keyboard and mouse) and what not to touch (everything else). Children keep a record of which of them have used programs by ticking their names on a class list by the computer. Establishing rules and procedures as part of the classroom environment has paid off in that the children are now largely independent when using simple programs.

Training for teachers at key stage 1: the future

The training of key stage 1 teachers has been rather inconsistent. The New Opportunities Fund (NOF) training – made available to schools several years ago – had a very patchy impact due to the varied nature of the training on offer. Although many teachers received good relevant training, many did not, and consequently some teachers still feel under-confident about their own ICT skills and lack confidence in integrating ICT into other subject areas. The future of training in this crucial curriculum area is outlined in the recently published policy document on the future of ICT in education, *Fulfilling the Potential: Transforming Teaching and Learning through ICT in Schools* (DfES 2003a). In the section on working towards an 'e-confident school' training is highlighted as a priority. The paper outlines an 'offer' of training which is based around Advanced Skills Teachers (ASTs), the identification and dissemination of effective practice, and the mobilisation of the 'national strategies field force' to promote and progress the use of ICT in teaching and learning. This is planned to begin with key stage 3, but to be rolled out to the other key stages in time. This approach relies on the expansion of existing professional development networks; in primary schools this is likely to be through ASTs and literacy and numeracy strategy advisers from the LEA. The hope is that in utilising the success of the existing relationships with schools, the problem of training which fails to meet needs, much encountered in the NOF-funded training, will be avoided.

Connectivity, hardware and software at key stage 1

There is a wide range of ICT resources available to suit key stage 1 children. Some programs such as Textease, Clicker and the RM version of Word, are specifically designed to introduce children to basic interfaces of software and operations such as opening, saving and printing files. These 'content-free' applications can be used across the curriculum to support learning. There is also an increasing range of software which has curriculum content, such as CDs and material available over the Internet. Providers are beginning to use video, images and sound to effectively create learning materials suitable for children who are at the early stages of being able to read. Broadband connectivity means that Internet-based resources can now be used effectively within lessons.

Key stage 2

Kelly Jones' first teaching job is in year 5 at Hillways, a large urban junior school. She has a class base and shares a large teaching area outside the classroom with the other two year 5 classes. The school has chosen to pool its resources, so instead of having computers in each class, it has chosen to put them all in a 'suite' in this area. There are 20 computers. Today the children in Kelly's class are using

'Logo' to explore angles as part of their numeracy work. They are working in pairs to make a variety of shapes.

Kelly uses video and music on CD regularly in her teaching. As part of her Newly Qualified Teacher (NQT) year, Kelly is working with the current ICT subject leader to develop her interest and skills in ICT, and she is hoping to take a share in the ICT subject leader role next year. As part of this, she is looking at the Qualifications and Curriculum Authority (QCA) scheme of work for science, and rewriting it for the school with ICT opportunities in mind.

Considering this situation, what are the ICT issues?

Key stage 2 curriculum and assessment, SATs and the Primary Strategy

Hillways uses the QCA schemes of work as a basis for their planning. These schemes have been variously criticised by many as being dull, vague, unrealistic, over-ambitious and confusing. However, for many teachers they have been helpful in planning at the medium and short term for a range of subjects, especially those they feel less confident in. However, as a result of the Primary Strategy, many schools are re-examining the use of the schemes. This is an excellent opportunity to consider how ICT in all its forms might be included in the scheme and subject leaders can make this a focus of their role.

Many primary schools feel pressure from the end of key stage SATs in year 6 (and some even in year 5!). The SATs do not contain an element of ICT use, as schools' opportunities and facilities differ so much. However ICT can play a role in preparation for the SATs, with revision materials available on the web, such as those on the BBC revisewise site.

Training at key stage 2, for a newly qualified teacher

Kelly is fortunate in having recently completed her initial teacher training, which had a significant element of ICT. Not only did she have to pass the ICT skills test in order to attain qualified teacher status (QTS), but she also undertook a regular audit of her skills as part of her course. There was a focus on her use of ICT in other subjects, both in the practical assessments made of her teaching and in the written portfolio compiled during her course. The focus on the use of ICT as a teaching and learning tool is the focus of several of the standards for initial teacher training as published by the Teacher Training Agency (TTA 2003a).

All trainees, whatever their route into teaching, must meet these standards about teaching and learning using ICT by the end of the training period. However, levels of confidence and competence in ICT are varied among NQTs. This is as a result of the varied experiences that trainees encounter in the schools where they undertake their training. These inconsistencies further highlight the need for support during the induction year and beyond.

Connectivity, hardware and software at key stage 2: The whole-school issues

The range of hardware and software available for primary schools is expanding, as outlined above. Better connectivity, better designed content and a wider range of input devices from rollerballs to tablet PCs are making ICT more accessible throughout the primary age range. This means that schools are faced increasingly with choices about what to invest in and how to organise it. In the past, a computer in each classroom was seen as a target, but with pupil–computer ratios increasingly heading towards the target of 8:1, schools are making strategic decisions about how to best achieve this, be it by locating more computers in classrooms, or by saving to install a suite of computers, or purchasing a trolley of laptops or tablets which can be transferred from room to room. Additionally, there is a wide range of peripherals such as scanners, cameras and dataloggers which enhance the use of ICT throughout the curriculum.

Key stage 3

Ken Fotheringham is a teacher of mathematics at Broadview High School. He is second in department and oversees key stage 3. In the school, children are grouped into four bands, according to ability. This is measured by an online assessment which Ken has developed using the WebCT Virtual Learning Environment (VLE). In their first mathematics lesson in the school, each class sits the test in the ICT suite, and the VLE collates and analyses the results. Although the test took a while to set up and develop, the electronic marking in the long run did save time and effort in the department. Ken is an enthusiast for ICT, but remains sceptical that ICT can really play a significant role in his teaching, instead viewing it as another useful resource.

Ken is keen to develop a range of teaching modes within key stage 3 in the school which match the pupils' learning styles. He promotes a varied approach, which includes direct interaction, didactic teaching and an enquiry-based approach. He has been using materials produced by the Department for Education and Skills to develop lesson planning and inclusion in the department (DfES 2004a; DfES 2004d). These materials have focused the department on meeting the needs of all their learners, and they have found that changes made thusfar have increased levels of motivation and also contributed to improved attendance in mathematics lessons. Ken's approach to using ICT as a tool in teaching has also contributed to improving pupil motivation, as skills and knowledge acquired during sessions have been beneficial to those proposing to follow either an academic or vocational route at key stage 4.

In a recent successful lesson, Ken's pupils designed a spreadsheet to solve a problem related to points in a football league. The question set was 'Would it be better for five football teams, given their current results, to have four points for a win and two for a draw, or three points for a win and one for a draw?' The pupils calculated the points scored by each team, given their results and comprised a scoring system which produced a range of versions of the league table. More able pupils devised a scoring system of their own to favour their favourite team. Ken is careful in his lesson planning to focus on maths objectives, however sometimes he finds his teaching time in lessons like these 'hijacked' by pupils needing to learn ICT skills. At Broadview High there are some ICT specialist teachers, but these teachers mainly work with key stage 4 pupils.

Considering this situation, what are the ICT issues?

Key stage 3 curriculum and assessment

Key stage 3 became the focus of educational change and development, with the inception of the key stage 3 strategy. Since then, this stage of education has been the focus of both professional development and a number of initiatives aimed at bridging the gap between the end of primary school and the challenges of key stage 4. The framework for teaching ICT capability has sought to support and develop pupils' specific ICT skills while there is also a focus on developing the use of ICT throughout the curriculum, especially in the core subjects. Schools have worked towards developing their schemes of work accordingly, and while improvements in standards as measured in SATs are small, they do provide a basis for future development. One of the main themes of the strategy and associated material is inclusion. In the first three years of the strategy, standards as measured by SATs and the numbers of pupils achieving level 5 had risen.

- In English the number of pupils achieving level 5 or above has increased by four percentage points, to 69 per cent in 2003.
- In mathematics the number of pupils achieving level 5 or above has increased by five percentage points, to 71 per cent in 2003.
- Results in science and ICT have also improved since the introduction of these strands in 2002. Science has increased by two percentage points too, to 68 per cent in 2003. ICT has increased by one percentage point, to 67 per cent in 2003.

(DfES, Key Stage 3 National Strategy Guide)

In 2004/5 the strategy has been examined and refocused on four key themes (DfES 2004e):

- Assessment for learning (AfL)
- ICT across the curriculum
- Literacy across the curriculum (LAC), and
- Leading in learning (learning and thinking skills).

This should mean that ICT continues to be focus of key stage 3 curriculum development.

Training at key stage 3: Continuing professional development in schools

The current teacher recruitment and retention debate, particularly relevant at secondary school level and in shortage subjects such as science, mathematics and modern foreign languages, revolves around the issue of workload. This is not simply an issue of the workload of 'ordinary' teachers, but increasingly that of those who also have teaching and learning responsibilities. In short, the amount which teachers are expected to have responsibility for has continued to increase, and despite legislation and support from the unions, not a great deal has been removed from the list of responsibilities of the teacher.

This means that every working moment of a teacher's day must be accounted for, and teachers must make difficult decisions about what to prioritise. A cynic might characterise current developments at key stage 3 as 'initiative overload'. It is fair to say that many of these initiatives are focused on improving standards of teaching and learning, but it is also felt that these initiatives have somewhat overtaken schools' own professional development agendas. When asked 'What would improve your ability to integrate ICT into your teaching?' most teachers reply, 'Time'. That is time to try ideas, time to work with colleagues from their own schools and other schools, time to rewrite schemes of work accordingly and to fully understand the potential of the ICT resources they have at their disposal. It is to be hoped that the government's current plans for the development of ICT (DfES 2003a) will enable schools and teachers to have this 'time', so they may develop really worthwhile ICT in their teaching.

Another problem related to professional development and teacher training affecting this school is the shortage of ICT specialist teachers, and so the dependence on teachers of other curriculum areas to deliver either specific ICT lessons or teach ICT skills in other curriculum areas. The issue of recruitment is dealt with in more detail in the key stage 4 section below.

Connectivity, hardware and software at key stage 3

Most secondary schools in the UK now have at least a two megabyte (2MB) broadband connection to the Internet. This means that reasonably fast Internet connection to the web is available to the desktop in computer suites and for stand-alone machines. Increasingly, these computers are connected to wireless networks which are adding to the portability of equipment such as laptops around the school. Wider bandwidth in the future should bring faster and increasingly reliable access to both the school network and the Internet in secondary schools.

Behind this is the development of Internet-based learning products for schools. This is often effectively curriculum content packaged and delivered via the network. In some cases this is free for schools. The range and quality of resources developed by the BBC means that this is often the first stop for teachers in search of resources to use in lessons. From the revision materials delivered for key stage 3 SATs and GCSEs to the extensive resources in the history and science sections, sometimes linked to television series, the BBC has made a significant contribution in this area. In addition schools now have available 'e-learning credits' which they can spend on digital resources. Companies like Espresso (www.espresso.co.uk) and Proquest (www.proquestlearning.co.uk) are producing materials which in the future may be available over the broadband network and via the Internet portals of the regional broadband consortia.

In addition to this 'content-based' software, pupils at key stage 3 increasingly make use of software such as word processors and spreadsheets to support and present what they have learned. Increasingly pupils have access to computers outside school, either in the home or in afterschool learning clubs provided by organisations such as libraries, football clubs and youth support organisations. They use these in producing homework and in researching and following up learning.

Teenagers treat technology as an integral part of their lives. Even ten years ago, it would have been hard to predict the ways in which teenagers use communication devices such as mobile phones and the Internet as a way to play games and socialise. Photos shared by phone, playing football on games consoles against someone in another town, having friends they'll never meet except in cyberspace are all real aspects of the life of a teenager. Increasingly this is putting pressure on schools to recognise this aspect of children's lives. However, this also raises the spectre of safety. Much has been written about the issue of Internet safety, some of it quite alarmist. But to try to prevent children communicating in these ways could be seen as pointless. What many schools are now recognising is that part of the education of pupils in using electronic communication of all forms is to teach them how to use it safely. The NSPCC has contributed significantly to resources in this area (NSPCC 2005).

Key stage 4 modern foreign languages

Olivia Connolly is a teacher of modern foreign languages (MFL) at the Huckerby High School in a large market town. She has worked in state schools for 20 years and was always an enthusiastic user of technology in her teaching. From the beginning of her career, she used 'language labs' to utilise audio cassettes and schemes to support her teaching. These labs have gradually been replaced by computer suites. Language labs have been effective in some ways, although buying suitable software for the expanding range of courses and languages her department is offering is problematic. In addition, the Internet connection, which she uses to enable her pupils to connect to suitable websites, is not always stable. Now Olivia has been given an interactive whiteboard to use in her teaching. These developments, however, are not the only changes Olivia has had to contend with in her 20-year career. In addition to curriculum, examinations and technology changing, in the early twenty-first century the whole nature of the 14–19 curriculum is undergoing significant scrutiny and change. Some may say that this phase of the educational system is suffering from inertia and is in need of development, hence annual calls by the press for 'something to be done' about the examinations system which happens annually around the time of the GCSE results being published in August.

The Tomlinson Report, which in 2002 created a significant controversy by calling for a complete rethink of the A level system followed by the setting up of a working group within the DfES on Curriculum and Qualifications Reform (DfES 2004f) headed up by Tomlinson, added to this perception. The report's recommendations remain far from fully enacted at the time of writing in 2005, however, if asked, most of those who actually work and teach in this phase would not agree that the phase is in stagnation. To the contrary, there are a number of initiatives underway in both curriculum and technology which are significantly affecting the sector, not least in modern foreign languages. Many teachers and managers support this reform (Bawden 2005) despite the impact of changes on their workload and professional status.

Olivia has seen her department suffer from a recruitment crisis and, while other departments at Huckerby High have expanded, MFL has the same number of teachers as it did ten years ago, and new posts have proved difficult to fill. As a proportion of the student body, fewer pupils take GCSEs in French and German than they did ten years ago, and even the introduction of newer languages such as Urdu and Chinese have failed to halt this proportional decrease. Huckerby High experiences problems which are not unusual in the secondary sector of pupil disaffection and problems with behaviour of pupils. All these factors affect Olivia's teaching role in a number of ways.

In her GCSE classes, Olivia has a wide range of pupils. The pupils for whom she has predicated GCSE grades A*–C are following an academic route through the school, and most of these pupils, Olivia hopes, will go on to further and higher education. She sees part of her role as supporting these pupils in developing not only the knowledge and skills they will need to pass their GCSEs, but also encouraging them to enjoy languages and see their importance, in the hope that many of them will continue to study languages. In some other classes, where she hopes pupils may achieve C grades, but in reality are more likely to achieve D–G grades, Olivia supports pupils in developing skills in a language which might help them in future vocational study. During breaks from teaching Olivia supports a number of pupils on a one-to-one basis in completing GCSE coursework, as well as playing a role in the department mentoring colleagues and supporting them in managing behaviour of more difficult pupils, some of whom seem to struggle to see the relevance of learning another language in a world dominated by, as they see it, an English-speaking media. And in addition to all this, Olivia has to find a way to use her new interactive whiteboard profitably in her teaching.

Considering this situation, what are the ICT issues?

On the face of it, Olivia's concerns about software, Internet connections and her new interactive whiteboard, in her day-to-day teaching, seem superficial when placed in the context of the pedagogical, curriculum and examination changes the 14–19 curriculum (DfES 2005b). Yet the solutions to some of Olivia's issues, as raised in the chapter, might very well be in the use of information technology.

ICT and the future of examinations: Curriculum and assessment at key stage 4

The present curriculum, qualifications and examinations system for 14–19 year olds has enabled more young people to gain the five good GCSEs employers consider essential for most jobs today, and allowed increasing numbers to go to university.
But teachers, lecturers and trainers know it also has significant weaknesses:

- There is too much assessment. Many teachers, lecturers and trainers feel that the current mix of coursework and formal assessment means that students have too many external exams, crowding out other activities.
- The system is confusing and unclear. There are too many qualifications and specifications.
- Bad behaviour makes teaching difficult. Truancy and bad behaviour, particularly among 14–16 year olds, can reflect restricted or inappropriate course options for some students.
- Too few young people continue learning beyond compulsory schooling. The UK has the fifth highest drop out rate at 16 among 28 of the world's most developed nations.
- Too few young people are properly equipped for work. Too few school-leavers can communicate, use number or use ICT effectively. Too few vocational qualifications meet the needs of learners and employers.

(DfES 2004f)

Enthusiasts for ICT, such as myself, can see a major role for ICT in this agenda as set out in the 14–19 working group's final report. Particularly when considering the three issues discussed below, ICT could have a significant effect. In some ways these issues relate to Olivia's concerns about computer suites, software, connectivity and interactive whiteboards, but in many ways this future agenda goes way beyond her current concerns.

Pupils need to leave school with an increasing range of ICT skills

Pupils experience an ever-widening range of ICT in schools, and pupils are increasingly confident in using the ICT they will use in the world of work. There has, however, been some speculation that the use of ICT in teaching and learning can also affect pupils' creative and critical thinking skills. In a recent systematic review (EPPI 2003) studies drawing links between computer teaching and assessment materials and creative and critical thinking skills were analysed. Although many of the studies did not offer systematic or quantitative evidence of such links, many of the studies found a qualitative relationship between some kinds of ICT use and creative and critical skills which employers value.

ICT use is motivational for pupils

Evidence for the motivational impact of ICT on pupils is well-established. In the DfES study *The big pICTure* (DfES 2003b), several studies are analysed and it is boldly stated that:

> Findings from several recent studies indicate that ICT can play an important role in motivating pupils and encouraging them to engage in learning within and beyond the classroom. Considering the importance of pupil motivation as a factor in pupil behaviour and attendance, both issues of significance as raised by the 14–19 review, and the weight of evidence building about motivation, it seems that this is a very important factor for KS4.

ICT has the power to streamline and simplify assessment procedures

Computer-based assessment is a controversial issue. Assessment in the form of external exams dominates the nature of key stage 4 education, and for computer aided assessment to become a significant factor would take considerable resources in terms of time, expertise and money. In a recent extensive literature review commissioned by Nesta Futurelab, the authors point out that the increasing use of ICT in lessons contrasts sharply with an examination system which is pen and paper based. They regard this restriction as 'bizarre' (Ridgeway and McCusker 2004). However they also concede that some models of computer-based assessment, especially those prevalent in the high school sector in the USA have not resulted in real gains being made. If real progress is to be made the authors warn against the 'dumbing down' (Ridgeway and McCusker 2004) of assessment. It seems that current research backs the use of assessment modes such as e-portfolios, where pupils can produce and collect a range of work which builds up a real picture of their knowledge and skills.

Recruitment and ICT: Professional development in shortage subjects at key stage 4

Recent years have witnessed a decline in the number of MFL teachers in secondary schools. Languages have joined sciences and mathematics on the list of 'shortage subjects', in which schools have found it hard to fill vacancies with suitable candidates. The Training and Development Agency for Schools (TDA) has recently launched an initiative to recruitment drive (TDA 2005). Current government ICT policy, as set out by the DfES in *Fulfilling the Potential* (DfES 2003a), points to ICT which should mean:

- revitalised professional networks supporting communication and collaboration, including the sharing of resources and best practice, within and between schools;
- support for workforce remodelling through the automation of routine administrative tasks and the availability of technical support.

(DfES 2003a)

In this way, it is hoped that the professional role of teachers will be made easier through the use of ICT, both in terms of teaching and learning and administration. This should have a positive impact on teacher retention levels in all subjects, including shortage subjects like MFL.

Key stage 5 science

Meg Waterfield is a teacher at Owen Glendower High in a large Welsh town. For the past two years, her school has been trailing the new 14–19 diploma or 'baccalaureate' qualification, alongside ordinary A levels. Meg teaches A level chemistry, as well as key stage 3 and GCSE science. Although Meg broadly supports the aims of the 14–19 agenda, she recognises that in practice, not all pupils have found the baccalaureate helpful in their progress towards further or higher education. While the course widened pupils learning both in terms of study and the vocational element, some pupils felt it was an additional pressure and was sometimes in conflict with their A level studies. Meg hopes to contribute in some way to the formal evaluation of the project.

In the meantime the day-to-day pressures of teaching science at A level continue. Meg is keen to involve individual pupils as much as possible in sharing their ideas and research with the whole group, and asks pupils to make PowerPoint presentations in order to demonstrate their understanding. This seemingly simple task requires pupils to take digital photographs, use datalogging equipment, produce an Excel spreadsheet and then collate this into a presentation. The pressures of A level study mean that Meg has very little time to teach the pupils the ICT skills they need to do all of this. Pupils' skills are variable, not just because her A level classes are of increasingly diverse ability, but also because the 'sixth form' (as it is still somewhat nostalgically referred to) is made up of pupils from a number of local schools, whose experience in ICT has differed widely.

Meg also has her eye on the future of her sixth form pupils. Some will go into higher education, one or two to high-powered medical courses. Others will use their qualifications towards getting points to study courses in further education which are outside the realm of science. She constantly tries to balance her teaching between the diverse needs of these groups and the many pupils whose needs fall somewhere in between. She hopes to use ICT as a tool for differentiating what she offers.

Curriculum at key stage 5: Meeting the needs of diverse learners

In the last ten years, a discussion about how schools prepare pupils for the world of work has raged among educationalists and industrialists. It has been a matter of debate as to whether the skills and knowledge with which young people leave school should be traditionally academic, or based on basic skills such as numeracy and literacy, or perhaps even include problem solving and thinking skills. John Abbott, the president of the Twenty-First Century Learning initiative writes in his book *The Unfinished Revolution*, of the way he perceives the problems in the education sector:

> The human brain and children's learning does not correspond to the mechanical blueprints of the industrial age... (a) new purpose for education, in contrast to a singular emphasis on discussions about systematic issues around academic success, should now focus on our best understandings of how the individual brain most effectively learns and takes control of future opportunities.
>
> (Abbott and Ryan 2000)

To what extent teachers subscribe to this 'new purpose in education' may be debatable, and undoubtedly issues relating to time, resources and teacher shortages would be raised even by those who subscribed to the theory. However we can see the beginnings of a response to the issues raised by Abbott in the final report of the Tomlinson committee (DfES 2004f). The strategy acknowledges in its justification for the need for reform that:

> Too few young people continue learning beyond compulsory schooling. The UK has the fifth highest drop out rate at 16 among 28 of the world's most developed nations.
> Too few young people are properly equipped for work. Too few school-leavers can communicate, use number or use ICT effectively. Too few vocational qualifications meet the needs of learners and employers.

Matching the content and teaching methods of the curriculum to the needs of employers and providing the right kind of education which encourages pupils to continue in education beyond 16 is, perhaps, the most significant challenge currently facing the secondary education sector.

Looking for support from the sphere of ICT in meeting this challenge is far from straightforward. In a Nesta Futurelab report on digital technologies and the 14–19 agenda (Davies, Hayward, *et al.* 2005), the authors fail to find significant evidence that digital technologies can have a positive effect on the education of this group. In the four case studies in the report, some small-scale positive effects are recorded, but the report concludes by calling for more research into this area on a much larger scale.

Schools, LEAs and teachers may, however, be assisted in meeting the challenges of the 14–19 agenda by ICT in the form of the potential of virtual learning. The conclusions in the futurelab report call for more research into:

- technologies which can combine with existing pedagogies;
- encouraging independence and collaboration in learning;
- benefiting those who might be educationally disadvantaged;
- meeting the specific needs of all learners.

At its best, virtual learning, through Virtual Learning Environments (VLEs) and Managed Learning Environments (MLEs) (see Chapter 6), has the potential support all of these. While development of VLEs is in its early stages in most schools at the time of writing, this is an area of ICT development which is under expansion. The BECTA research summary (BECTA 2003) on virtual learning environments identifies a body of research which suggests that VLEs can support face-to-face teaching and learning skills such as promoting self study, peer collaboration and presentational skills. There are currently fewer studies which would support the idea that VLEs might be of benefit to the educationally disadvantaged or promote individualised learning which meets the specific needs of learners. However, the conclusions of the report speculate that VLEs might support 'minority subjects' and be used to give 'extra support' to individual learners. As virtual learning moves forward, the development of managed learning environments which, by combining administrative and teaching systems, should streamline virtual learning and make it even more accessible and useful to teachers and learners.

Assessment at key stage 5 – the diploma. Where can ICT support this initiative?

The final report of the Tomlinson working Group on 14–19 Reform (DfES 2004f) sets out the blueprint for the proposed diploma format which is hoped will replace the existing GCSEs, BTECs, AVCEs, AS and A levels. The content of the diploma is devised between specialisms in academic or vocational subjects, core learning, focusing on what might be loosely termed 'basic' skills. Despite the difficulties which have become apparent in the qualification during the Wales based piloting of the project (Press Association 2005) the diploma looks as if it will continue to develop over the next ten years. Although, as discussed above, there is still little tangible research to link ICT and virtual learning. The *14–19 Gateway* website (DfES 2005d) cites several projects where ICT has significantly contributed to projects which pilot innovation in this phase. Among these small-scale but illuminating projects is the 'blended learning' in a high school in Derbyshire (Broadhead 2005) where the teachers have successfully 'blended' virtual and traditional face-to-face learning to the benefit of pupils. Whether this project or others like it really demonstrate that ICT has a pivotal role in the development of 14–19 teaching, learning and assessment may be questionable, but there are certainly signs that ICT is playing a role as the 14–19 project progresses.

ICT and the twenty-first-century educational society

Keeping up with developments in education, even for the most committed and enthusiastic teacher is difficult and keeping up with developments in ICT even more so. In these fast moving worlds, may teachers feel pressured by, worried by, and even 'left behind' by the speed of change. However in the UK we still are lucky enough to have a teaching workforce which is committed to enabling pupils to do their best.

In order to maintain teachers' focus on changes in the educational agenda and in ICT, we must persuade them that these changes have the best interest of their pupils at heart. And in this lies the problem. ICT has very much still to prove its worth in schools. Despite substantial research into and resources being invested in ICT in schools, we are still looking for the proverbial 'silver bullet' which shows us that ICT can really benefit learning.

Progress in ICT in teaching and learning has been surprisingly rapid. Only 20 years before the writing of this book, ICT was in its infancy in schools. Now, in 2005, looking at these vignettes, we can see that ICT is an important element of teachers' and pupils' daily lives in schools. ICT is certainly here to stay. The rest of this book examines in detail how teachers can make progress in using ICT in their teaching and learning by overcoming barriers and identifying the benefits of ICT.

References

Abbott, J. and Ryan, T. (2000) *The Unfinished Revolution*. Stafford, Network Educational Press.

Bawden, A. (2005) 'Calls for government to speed up 14 to 19 reform' in *Guardian Unlimited*.

BECTA (2003) *What the Research Says about Virtual Learning Environments*. BECTA, Coventry.

Broadhead, E. (2005) *Blended Learning at Lady Manners School Derbyshire 14–19 Pathfinder*. DfES, London.

Davies, C., Hayward, G., Lukman, L. (2005) *14–19 and Digital Technologies: A Review of Research and Projects*. Nesta Futurelab, Bristol.

DfEE and QCA (1999) *The National Curriculum. Handbook for Primary Teachers in England. Key Stages 1 and 2*. DfEE and QCA, London.

DfEE and QCA (2000) *Curriculum Guidance for the Foundation Stage*. DfEE and QCA, London.

DfES (2003a) *Fulfilling the Potential: Transforming Teaching and Learning Through ICT in Schools*. DfES, London.

DfES (2003b) *The big pICTure: The Impact of ICT on Attainment, Motivation and Learning*. DfES, London.

DfES (2004a) *Pedagogy and Practice: Teaching and Learning in Secondary Schools Unit 4: Lesson Design for Inclusion*. DfES, London.

DfES (2004d) *Pedagogy and Practice: Teaching and Learning in Secondary Schools Unit 1: Structuring Learning*. DfES, London.

DfES (2004e) *The Standards Site: The Key Stage 3 Strategy*. DfES, London.

DfES (2004f) *14–19 Curriculum and Qualifications Reform*. DfES, London.

DfES (2005b) *14–19 Education and Skills Summary*. DfES, London.

DfES (2005d). *14–19 Gateway*. DfES, London.

DfES. Key Stage 3 National Strategy Guide: www.standards.dfes.gov.uk/keystage3/.

EPPI (2003) *A Systematic Review of the Impact on Students and Teachers of the Use of ICT for Assessment of Creative and Critical Thinking Skills*. EPPI, London.

Harrison, C., Comber, C., Fisher, T., Haw, K., Lewin, C., Luzner, E., McFarlane, A., Mavers, D., Scrimshaw, P., Somekh, B., Watling, R. (2002) *ImpaCT2: The Impact of Information and Communication on Pupil Learning and Attainment. Strand 1 Report*. DfES, London.

NSPCC (2005) http://www.nspcc.org.uk/html/home/home.htm.

Press Association (2005) 'Baccalaureate drop out rate tops 50 per cent' in *Guardian Unlimited*.

Ridgeway, J. and McCusker, S. (2004) *Literature Review of E-assessment*. Nesta Futurelab, Bristol.

TDA (2005) News release – 'Voulez-vous parler Francais? – then become a modern languages teacher', Training and Development Agency for schools.

TTA (2003a) *Qualifying to Teach. Handbook of Guidance*. Summer. TTA, London.

CHAPTER 2

The barriers in learning technology procurement

Background and introduction: How procurement affects teaching and learning

Since the first computers were bought and installed in schools in the 1980s, the proportion of the education budget spent on Information and Communications Technology (ICT) has grown substantially. Along with this, The Department for Education and Skills (DfES) and Local Education Authorities (LEAs) have become increasingly involved in the process of procuring what schools need to deliver ICT effectively. This however has led to a conflict between the larger organisations being able to offer economies of scale (which helps schools get more for their money) and schools' autonomy and wish to choose their own ways of providing ICT which best fits their own circumstances. There is no simple way to resolve this conflict.

A key question raised in relation to the funding of ICT in schools is whether the amount of money spent on ICT is justified by the improvement in pupil attainment. In short, is ICT worth what it costs?

The *ImpaCT2* (Harrison, Comber, *et al.* 2002) study sought to tackle the issue of how to measure the impact of ICT on teaching and learning, examining both methodologies and data on ICT in schools. Strand one of the report focuses on statistics on pupil attainment from a wide range of pupils in English, Mathematics and Science at key stages 2, 3 and 4. Its key findings were:

- Differences in attainment associated with the greater use of ICT were clearly present in more than a third of all comparisons made between pupils' expected and actual scores in National Tests or GCSEs, though these were not large.
- In none of the comparisons was there a statistically significant advantage to groups with lower ICT use.

Those who are sceptical about the benefits of ICT in schools and flag carriers for computers in schools will interpret these findings very differently.

An ICT sceptic might assert that if improvements in attainment are only clearly present in 'more than a third' (not even half!) of the cases, this statistic shows that money being spent on ICT is failing to have a positive impact on the learning of most pupils. A sceptic might go on to ask if a similar amount of money was spent on extra teachers, buildings or resources such as books, and whether this might very well have a greater impact on pupil attainment. The substantial amount of money being spent on ICT in schools, figures for 2005/6 indicate that over £700 million will be spent on ICT in schools in England (DfES 2003a) makes this question even more important. In short, the investment in ICT is huge and the benefits are not yet being demonstrated in improved attainment in the majority of pupils.

However, to explore the other side of the argument, those who enthuse about the benefits of ICT would argue that in this case we need to continue to invest in ICT over a number of years in order to see more extensive benefits than are indicated in *ImpaCT2*. In other words, these who are enthusiastic about ICT would argue that the investment in ICT is a gamble worth taking. It may be argued that we are relatively early on in finding out and developing the role of ICT in our schools, and that the investment being made now in high-speed connections, hardware, support and training will sooner or later pay dividends in pupil attainment. In addition, these flag carriers may also cite the second key finding of *ImpaCT*, in that lower ICT use did not have a positive effect on grades either. In addition there are a range of justifications for the spending on ICT including the need to prepare pupils to use ICT in the world of work, the benefits of ICT systems on teacher workload and the ability of ICT to widen access to education for those with special needs, or who are isolated either in time or geographically. For these reasons, flag carriers for ICT would argue that raised pupil attainment is just one of the benefits of ICT, which can enhance schools in so many other ways.

Whether you are sceptic or a flag carrier, though, one thing is for certain. For the next few years ICT is here to stay in schools, and so LEAs, governors, headteachers and teachers must make decisions about how best to spend the money available.

Aims of this chapter

The introduction to this chapter begins with the central controversy of funding ICT in schools – whether ICT provides value for money. However this is not the only difficult or controversial issue in the funding of ICT in schools. Whether control should be central or devolved to schools and how much should be contributed at central and local levels also raises difficult questions. The aim of this chapter is to explore these issues in order to help the reader gain an understanding of the process, and crucially how different funding decisions might impact on ICT provision at the classroom level.

Definition of terms

Here is a list of those involved in the procurement process and their roles:

- British Educational Communications and Technology Agency (BECTA) – a government agency concerned with supporting ICT development in schools and colleges. www.becta.org.uk
- Regional Aggregation Bodies (RABs) – organisations in each are set up to enable co-ordination between National Health Service, Department of Trade and Industry and Regional Broadband Consortia to get the best out of broadband network development.
- Department for Education and Skills (DfES) – government department in charge of education.
- Local Education Authority (LEA) – local government body in charge of education in that area. Some LEAs cover large counties, others are small and cover only a London Borough or urban unitary area.
- National College for School Leadership (NCSL) – a body supporting the professional development of teachers in all areas of school management. www.ncsl.org.uk
- Schools – for the purposes of funding, defined as those nursery, primary and secondary schools in the state sector, educating pupils between the foundation stage and key stage 4. Private, voluntary sector and independent nurseries can apply to be included.

Terms and descriptions

Projects

- Computer to Pupil ratios – the ratios set up under the NGfL project as targets for the number of computers to schools. The ratios at the end of the NGfL project were 1:8 in the primary phase and 1:5 in the secondary phase.
- Curriculum Online – portal for the promotion of the eLC scheme.
- Hands on Support – a scheme to provide schools with technical and pedagogical support and training. Funded through standards fund and programmes are developed locally with schools and/or LEAs.
- ICT in Schools Programme (ICTiS) – programme to develop the role of ICT in schools, running between 2003 an 2006. The successor of the NGfL

project. The focus is on the pedagogy of ICT use and on whole school improvement.

- Laptops for Teachers (LfT) – a scheme to allow teachers 'personal access' to a laptop for curriculum and administration purposes. By 2006 two-thirds of teachers should have a laptop under this scheme.
- National Grid for Learning (NGfL) – Programme to develop the role of ICT in schools, running between 1998 and 2002. The focus was on infrastructure, connectivity and professional development.

Funding

- Devolved Capital Formula (DCF) – school funding which is based on a standard amount per school plus an amount per pupil. This can be rolled over for three financial years in order for schools to 'save up' for a project. This is funded by central government but the school must match the fund with 10 per cent of the total amount from existing budgets. This is one of the streams of funding from which schools may pay for ICT developments, along with Standards Fund.
- Standards Fund – a way of funding schools which is organised into grants for specific projects. A range of Standards Fund grants may be spent on ICT, for example, Grant 8, which is to support the development of the key stage three strategy. The main grant for ICT development is Grant 31, which has three strands. This is one of the streams of funding from which schools may pay for ICT developments, along with Developed Formula Capital.

ICT terms

- Asymmetric connection – a type of non broadband connection to the Internet (such as ADSL);
- Broadband connection – a connection to the Internet of more than 2 Mbps (Megabits per second);
- Cache – a store of Internet pages within the school or institution kept so the network doesn't have to go to the source every time the webpage is requested within the school;
- Connectivity – overall term for connection to a network and the Internet;
- Content Delivery Network Application Profile – BECTA checklist to assess a system's ability to deliver appropriate content at school, LEA and RBC level;
- Electronic Learning Credits (eLCs) – funding which schools can spend on CD-ROMs, DVDs, software and online services via the curriculum online website;
- Local Area Network (LAN) – the connections between computers in a school or institution. These may be wired or wireless.

Case studies

An examination of two cases studies follows. One looks at hardware (interactive whiteboards), the other at how support is funded (the 'Hands on Support' training initiative).

Buying hardware: Issues for schools

Since the National Grid for Learning initiative began in 1998, schools have been receiving substantial funds to spend on ICT hardware, software and support. Different schools and LEAs have made different decisions about spending this money. While some LEAs gave each school money for each year of the initiative, others gave schools a lump sum to enable them to buy more equipment at a better price. In addition some LEAs have given schools close guidance about their spending decisions; others have provided support only when requested. LEAs and schools have had difficult decisions to make in context. While schools may wish for the autonomy to purchase the ICT solutions which they perceive are best for their schools, LEAs may be able to supply expertise and crucial economies of scale which may be of benefit to all schools, especially small schools in the primary sector.

With the introduction of the Information and Communications Technology in Schools (ICTiS) initiative in 2003, the focus of spending on ICT changed in favour of 'Focus on ICT pedagogy and whole school improvement' (DfES 2003a). Part of this initiative is directed towards enabling schools to purchase electronic whiteboards. How and why this decision has been taken and what that means for schools is a good example of how ICT procurement might develop in the future.

As with all new technologies, when they were first introduced into schools in the late 1990s, interactive whiteboards were temperamental technology. Essentially the hardware consists of a large whiteboard which is either on trolley or attached to a wall, and a data projector. These are connected into a loop with a computer (most schools use laptops for this but it's not essential). The whiteboard is sensitive to the touch of a pen, or anything else, on the screen, and the whiteboard becomes like a large touch screen for the computer. It is possible to use software which also enables the user to 'write' on the board, using either a pen or a finger, to alter and add to the image projected.

In 2003, BECTA commissioned some research into the effectiveness of interactive whiteboards as a tool for teaching and learning (BECTA 2003). The findings indicate that they can have a positive effect on teaching and learning, in terms of allowing pupils to interact more in lessons, allowing teachers to make good use of web-based resources. In addition their use is motivational, according to some studies. The research is less clear about whether these benefits could be matched if schools simply installed data projectors and ordinary whiteboards, at roughly half the cost. There is some research into activities which can only be done using an interactive whiteboard, such as the saving and printing of notes made on the board, or the ability to make and generate text and images on the board, showing that this technology can, in some cases, enable teachers and pupils to work in new and innovative ways. However individual teachers, managers and researchers reflect on the usefulness of interactive whiteboard technology, their use is a focus of the ICTiS initiative and arrangements have been made for schools to purchase them. Guidance for schools and LEAs about Standards Fund Grant 31a details that schools should progressively equip more teaching areas with whiteboards, which can 'have great impact on pupil motivation and achievement' (DfES 2005).

Economy of scale is an important issue in ICT procurement. Establishing a system which effectively balances the needs of schools to purchase the equipment that suits them best against the financial benefits of bulk buying is difficult. In addition, rules established by the European Union require that where substantial amounts of public money are spent (such as bulk buying ICT equipment in this case) the process must be opened up for companies to tender for the business. In 2004, BECTA developed a system of whiteboard purchasing which fits with the EU requirements but allows schools to purchase whiteboards at substantial discount. Details of this scheme are available on a dedicated BECTA run website at http://www.whiteboards.becta.org.uk/, which enables schools to search for whiteboards provided by nine companies with different sizes and specifications of projection.

Considering this situation, schools have limited freedom about how they spend their money on hardware. Money given to schools by Grant 31a is earmarked for interactive whiteboards and if they are to get value for money, they should buy from the range supplied through the BECTA initiative. Not all hardware purchasing follows this model, but it may be that policy-makers will decide that in order to be cost effective in terms of gains in pupil attainment, ICT funds will be targeted to areas where research suggests gains can be made and purchasing through schemes such as the BECTA will provide some freedom for schools to get equipment that meets their needs while making the most of savings which come through bulk purchasing.

Summary of issues for schools in buying hardware

- Schools need to balance their autonomy to choose appropriate hardware and software for their needs against the bulk buying power of clusters of schools or LEAs.
- New technologies are constantly emerging.
- Money spent on new hardware and software isn't always value for money if schools are not utilising the full potential of their existing resources.

- New ways of getting value for money are emerging with a role for BECTA in procurement.

Paying for support: Issues for schools

A different approach to procurement is taken in relation to the 'Hands on Support' initiative. In *Fulfilling the Potential* (DfES 2003a) the aims and rationale of the programme of training and support are set out.

> The package of support for each subject area will be developed in conjunction with subject specialists, the subject associations and all the agencies involved in supporting subject teachers. It will include a free, national source of advice on, and support for, using ICT in teaching and learning as well as exemplification of how ICT capability can be applied and developed in a subject context, and will build on the work currently being done by BECTA, the QCA and the national strategies.
>
> (DfES 2003a)

This is manifested in the 'Hands on Support' initiative. Essentially LEAs and schools are required to work together to put together a programme of support which meets the needs of the school in terms of both professional development for teachers and technical support for ICT in schools. Schools may decide that their needs can be met by operating an in-house programme or they might decide to work with other schools or with the private sector if they wish.

The funding is through Grant 31a of the Standards fund, and LEAs are required to 'match fund' the amount given by central government. These funds may then be devolved to schools (with a small amount being kept by the LEA to cover administration) or some or all of it may be kept centrally should schools wish to work with the LEA to develop the Hands on Support programme.

The Hands on Support programme is also closely linked with existing initiatives such as the key stage 3 Strategy, the Primary Strategy and the use of Advanced Skills Teachers to support professional development in their area. Details of the programme can be found on the Teachernet website http://www.teachernet.gov.uk/wholeschool/ictis/ict_teaching/hos/.

This programme allows schools freedom to decide to opt in or out of a number of options, and although the funding still comes via the LEA, schools are under no obligation to work within a prescribed format to spend their money.

Summary of issues for schools in buying support

- The quality of Hands on Support initiative depends to some extent on the range and quality of what the LEA and other local providers are offering.
- As with many aspects of in school professional development, it is dependent on the personnel involved as well as the systems.

Issues raised

To what extent do the purchasing arrangements for interactive whiteboards represent a good use of resources?

On the face of it, the arrangements made for BECTA to evaluate whiteboards and then enable schools to benefit from buying them at a reduced rate seems like a sensible approach. There is much evidence to suggest that interactive whiteboards can have a very positive effect on teaching and learning. BECTA have collected together the findings of research projects (BECTA 2003).

Interactive whiteboards can:

- enable teachers to share electronic resources, including web-based resources effectively, and to demonstrate their use;
- enable teachers and pupils to add to an annotate resources for the whole class to see;
- give teachers access to technology that is relatively reliable and easy to use;
- support interactive and discursive approaches to teaching and learning;
- enable teachers to save and print notes made on the board;
- enable young and disabled pupils to interact with technology in a simple and accessible way.

As with many ICT devices, there is some evidence to suggest these are motivational for pupils and teachers.

Despite these findings however, there are also grounds for some scepticism about whether the substantial cost of interactive whiteboards is really justified in improved teaching and learning. The issue is simple, although there is some significant research into the area, it does not mean that interactive whiteboards are the best use of funds for all schools. It may be that the schools require the funding to update or support other ICT initiatives, and this is not taken into by these funding arrangements. In short, although the case for the usefulness if interactive whiteboards is made, they may still not be the funding priority for all schools.

To what extent are schools able to design Hands on Support solutions which meet the needs of their school?

Looking at the guidance for providers of the Hands on Support initiative the scheme is clear about what it sets out to do.

1.2 Principles of HOS

The HOS strategy is based on the following key principles:

- sharing good practice in the use of ICT to enhance teaching and learning;
- classroom based support for teachers, using equipment they are familiar with;
- differentiated support, suited to individual teachers' needs;
- support that goes beyond basic skills and technology, and which focuses on pedagogy to support more effective use of ICT in teaching and learning across all subjects and key stages; and
- releasing value from prior investment in ICT infrastructure, equipment, connectivity and training.

The central focus of HOS is using ICT effectively as part of teaching and learning. HOS is not about training teachers in ICT skills. It is about supporting colleagues in using ICT in teaching and learning.

HOS is not about:

- basic ICT skills training
- technical support
- school leadership training
- ICT as a discrete subject
- one size fits all.

(DfES 2004b; DfES 2004c)

The question raised is: To what extent does this arrangement represent value for money and effective use of funds? It seems from the guidance that the scheme avoids some of the pitfalls of its forerunner, the New Opportunities Fund (NOF) training scheme, which provided training, and was often badly matched to the needs of teachers because it didn't take account of what teachers knew and failed to account for the need to develop basic skills before pedagogical development was possible.

The flexibility built into the scheme, where schools can select how they buy their support should mean that schools can choose a solution which suits their needs and circumstances. Schools can purchase support from their LEA either individually or in clusters or design and deliver their own support. With the programme in its infancy at the time of writing, however, the signs that this support will prove to be good value for money judging by the documents published are promising.

As part of the Standards Fund Grant A there is also a provision for schools to purchase technical support for their ICT resources. They can use this money to either buy technical support via the LEA or by paying for their own technician.

BECTA supplies guidance for schools in this respect, however this issue remains a difficult one for schools, in trying to use the funds to meet their needs, especially small schools, who receive a relatively small amount of money and so can afford a technician only infrequently.

Barriers summarised: How different stakeholders perceive needs

Looking at the barriers to funding from the schools perspective, the main issue seems to be that schools have limited choice in how they spend the funds allocated for ICT resources. The arrangements for Standards Fund Grants mean that specific amounts are allocated to specific ICT areas.

Funding is not transferable between areas, except in the case of the Devolved Capital Formula (DCF). This can be seen to be a barrier to schools that need resources to be focused on a particular area. For example, if a school considers training a priority, it cannot spend the money allocated to e-learning credits on training. This means they may end up with more software to add to their collection, and insufficient resources to fund the training to use what they already have effectively. In addition where schools need to update existing hardware such as desktop computers, or move from desktops to laptops or tablets, they cannot spend the money they have allocated for whiteboards on the project.

Therefore this kind of ring-fencing of funds is a barrier to schools being able to meet their needs effectively from what they have available.

In addition, much of this funding must be matched by the LEA or the school in order to be accessed. It is more realistic to look at funds allocated by central government as an offer of funding, dependent on whether LEA and schools can match the funding. In the case of the Standards Fund Grant 31a, all the central funding must be matched by an equal amount of LEA money. This means that in order to make the best of their allocation, LEAs must prioritise funding from the education budget for ICT. It could be argued that this gives ICT an unfair priority over other education resources. The DCF funding stream must be matched by a 10 per cent 'governing body contribution' – effectively the school must find 10 per cent of the funding it wishes to access from other areas.

This kind of matched funding is another barrier to schools being able to fund their learning resources most effectively for their own situation.

Despite these problems for funding being ring-fenced and needing to be 'matched', levels of finance available for ICT are substantial. In the academic year 2005/6 total funds to be spent on ICT in England are in the region of £700 million. This is a multi-million pound business. Although much of this funding

Table 2.1 ICT funding sources

	Source	Priority	What the school gets
Infrastructure and Hands on Support	Standards Fund Grant 31a	Achieving and maintaining computer to pupil ratios	More computers: laptops/desktops/tablets
	Standards Fund Grant 31a	Providing schools with caching resources	A server with a caching facility
	Standards Fund Grant 31a	Hands on Support initiative	Training
	Standards Fund Grant 31a	Providing schools with interactive whiteboards and/or digital projectors	Whiteboards/projectors
	Standards Fund Grant 31a	Laptops for Teachers	Individual teachers may receive laptops
	Standards Fund Grant 31a	ICT technical support.	Some time from an ICT technician
Connectivity	Standards Fund Grant 31b	Providing Connectivity	Faster/more reliable Internet access
E-learning credits	Standards Fund Grant 31c	The purchase of online and local software resources	E-learning credits to spend via the curriculum online website
Projects	Developed Capital Formula	Schools can use this funding for ICT projects if they wish, and roll funds over for from year to year to fund small-scale capital work if necessary	No restrictions – whatever the project needs

is fed through LEAs and schools, a great deal of it ends up with large companies who have made a significant success from educational ICT products. These include:

- Research Machines (RM), who make PC platform desktops, laptops and tablets specifically designed for use in school, along with peripherals and software and even became involved in the NOF training project;
- Softease, who design and manufacture software for schools;
- Espresso, who design and deliver curriculum content for broadband networks;
- Logitron, who design and make peripherals such as dataloggers.

These are just examples of some of the companies who are working in the ICT for the education market.

In some ways this market can be seen as helpful to schools and supportive to teaching and learning. Where companies have produced products which have proved successful and useful they have grown in size and influence. But there are also those who would say that the ICT for education market is being led by companies who spend a lot of time enforcing what they think schools *should* have on busy schools who don't have the time and/or expertise to choose what really meets their needs best. As with all polemics, the truth of the matter probably lies somewhere in between. While these companies do promote their products to schools and continue to produce new and better solutions, their focus on educational ICT is certainly more helpful to schools than if they had to deal with companies who design and make ICT solutions for commerce and business. Most of these companies do employ significant numbers of trained teachers and people with real expertise in the field. In addition organisations like BECTA are now increasingly supporting teachers as a 'go-between' for these companies and schools and LEAs.

The ICT for Education marketplace is competitive and schools are often faced with many choices about how to spend their money. This may be a barrier to effective use of funds.

Overcoming the barriers and identifying benefits

Given these barriers, schools have to plan carefully and make informed choices about spending money on ICT. This section is designed to suggest some approaches to planning and making these choices. The aim is not to provide a magic formula to overcome the barriers, but to suggest some practical approaches towards getting the maximum benefits from the available resources.

BARRIER There is a wide range of stakeholders in the educational ICT market.

BENEFIT By identifying the roles of different stakeholders it is possible maximise the potential of ICT to have positive effect on teaching and learning.

Schools and LEAs in partnership

- Local Education Authorities may need to look at their strategic role in supporting schools, considering how best to meet the needs of all schools, whatever their size and phase. It seems likely that LEAs will continue to have a significant role to play, particularly in continuing professional development. Therefore, the role they are able to take in managing and leading the 'Hands on Support' initiative seems crucial.

- Headteachers may need to think in a strategic way about their budgets. Although much of the funding for ICT is ring-fenced, possibilities for rolling over funds through several years may mean that larger projects may be taken on.

- ICT subject leaders may need to carefully consider their role in the management of funds. The amount of influence ICT subject leaders have on spending issues varies from school to school, but ICT subject leaders need to be proactive in clearly identifying the needs of their schools as far as ICT provision and training goes. In addition it is likely that ICT subject leaders will increasingly have to assist the school management team by taking a strategic view of ICT development which is closely focused on teaching and learning.

- Teachers may need to assess their own needs in terms of professional development in ICT. This might be in terms of technical expertise, development of skills in planning to use ICT in their subjects, support in exploring teaching strategies which are successful, or in teaching ICT skills. Teachers need to work in teams to develop curricula and schemes of work which make good use of the ICT resources available in their schools.

- Pupils may need to work with their teachers on new ways of teaching and learning, and share their understanding and expertise in ICT with the whole school community.

- Parents may need to have an open-minded approach to the use of ICT in their children's school experience, and give support where they are able.

BARRIER Budgeting for all the needs of ICT including maintenance, training and running costs.

BENEFIT Careful financial planning for the 'total cost of ownership' of ICT can help maximise the potential of an investment in hardware and software.

Total cost of ownership

The issue of the total cost of ownership (TCO) of a piece of ICT equipment has recently been the subject of a literature review by BECTA (Scrimshaw 2002). Key findings of the report for schools and LEAs include the following:

- Schools must make a choice between purchasing ICT though a 'managed service' (where an LEA or company provide technical support) and dealing with a number of agencies to get technical support in an effort to get value for money from specialists.
- If TCO is going to be part of the overall ICT strategy for schools and LEAs more studies are needed into the principles (for example, how should teacher 'time' be factored in as a monetary cost) and practicalities (what is the cost of effective professional development for schools).
- Budgeted and unbudgeted costs can be difficult to define.

In principle the report finds evidence that is positive about the concept of TCO being a useful tool in future planning of ICT development by schools and LEAs. However, as the majority of the studies included in the literature review are based around models in industry, and the studies included which have an educational context are from the USA, there seems to be some work to be done before we can really say that there is a good understanding of the total cost of ownership of a computer in a school in the UK.

Planning for future needs

Given all of these difficult issues and barriers in ICT funding, a school manager, ICT subject leader, school governor or teacher could feel that planning for the future development of ICT in a school is an almost impossible task. Many of these stakeholders will feel that they have ideas about what they would like ICT to be able to do in the school. These are listed below. It is right that those most closely involved with teaching and learning in school should have a significant influence on policy, and it is these stakeholders who should maintain a focus of the objectives which are relevant to their own school and situation.

Objectives might include some of the following:

- ICT should support the learning development of all pupils.
- ICT should support all subjects in the curriculum, adapting to meet the needs of each subject; provisions should include subject-specific hardware and software where appropriate.
- ICT should support inclusion in schools – where an ICT device or piece of software can allow an individual access to an aspect of school life or learning they would not otherwise be able to access, every effort should be made to provide the necessary ICT.

- ICT should be integrated into the curriculum in ways which are useful to the subject.
- ICT should be integrated into the curriculum in ways which support the development of specific ICT skills in a systematic way.
- ICT should provide value for money.

Given these as objectives, stakeholders might plan for the development of ICT in a school in the short term (things which can be achieved in the current academic year), medium term (things which can be achieved in the space of the next two or three academic years), and long term (goals for the future). Given that it is impossible to know the future for ICT, in terms of funding and the possibilities of learning technology (see Chapter 4), medium and long-term objectives might well be less concrete and specific than short-term ones, but this should not preclude each school developing a vision for the future of ICT in each school.

Further reading and references: Comparisons and studies of various hardware and software systems

A chapter in a book such as this can do no more than take a broad sweep of the complex issues of the funding of ICT in schools. Further reading on this subject is available via a number of sources, including the British Educational Communications and Technology Agency (BECTA), government sources such as the Department for Education and Skills, businesses concerned with this market, and independent and academic sources. The following is by no means an exhaustive list of what is available, but follows through some of the main themes of this chapter.

Further reading about funding sources

As this chapter discusses, the arrangements for funding ICT in schools are complex. However the main streams of funding are detailed and explained on the Teachernet website at: www.teachernet.gov.uk/_doc/8055/SFGuidance%200405.doc.

This document, provides a usefully detailed description of the standard funds and grants, how they might be spent, and whether they are matched funded. In addition information can be found on the additional Developed Capital Formula funding stream by following the links from the Teachernet homepage www.teachernet.gov.uk through the ICT in Schools and Funding sections.

Further reading about the total cost of ownership

There are a number of studies about TCO, but most of these are based in a business context or in non-UK (mainly North American) schools. However the results of these have been distilled and examined in the BECTA literature review, in the form of a report to the DfES. The review both synthesises the findings of the available literature and discusses issues such as how TCO models might be practically applied in a school content, and strategies for obtaining TCO data.

Further reading about purchasing

Schools regularly receive 'junk mail' offering ICT products and services, so getting a picture of what is available is not difficult for a headteacher, subject leader or teacher. However making sense of these and comparing what's on offer and prices can be time-consuming. To some extent, however, this problem has been circumvented by the BECTA initiatives with whiteboards, where each product is detailed and explained and available through the single source. Information about this is available on the BECTA website at www.becta.org.uk.

Products are also available to be examined and even bought online. Research Machines (RM) run a particularly extensive website detailing their products and services. This can be used not only to purchase RM products but by teachers to compare prices and products from other companies (www.rm.com).

Further reading about training and support

The future of professional development is in the form of Hands on Support initiative. Documents and information for LEAs and other providers is available on the Teachernet website: http://www.teachernet.gov.uk/wholeschool/ictis/ict_teaching/hos/.

In addition there are two DfES publications available for providers. These give a useful outline of what providers can be expected to do and how they might do it, which may also be of interest to school managers and teachers.

References

BECTA (2003) *What the Research Says about Interactive Whiteboards*. BECTA, Coventry.

DfES (2003a). *Fulfilling the Potential: Transforming Teaching and Learning Through ICT in Schools*. DfES, London.

DfES (2004b) *Hands on Support. Guidance and Support for HOS Providers. Secondary*. DfES, London.

DfES (2004c) *Hands on Support. Guidance and Support for HOS Providers. Primary*. DfES, London.

DfES (2005) Teachernet website: http://www.teachernet.gov.uk/.

Harrison, C., Comber, C., Fisher, T., Haw, K., Lewin, C., Luzner, E.,McFarlane, A., Mavers, D., Scrimshaw, P., Somekh, B., Watling, R. (2002) *ImpaCT2: The Impact of Information and Communication on Pupil Learning and Attainment. Strand 1 Report*. DfES, London

Scrimshaw, P. (2002) *Total Cost of Ownership: A Review of the Literature*. DfES, London.

CHAPTER 3

The technical barriers to the use of learning technology

Background and introduction: Technology and progress

My first memories of using a computer come from my own school days. I vividly remember the thrill of programming a Sinclair ZX81 in computer club during my first years in secondary school. Looking back, my excitement at writing short programs in BASIC was a sure indicator that I was going to become a computer addict, a techie, in my later years. Shortly after this my parents bought our first home computer, a Sinclair ZX Spectrum. We played games on this, loading the programs via a tape recorder. At the time, few of the items in our mid-1980s family home would have contained a microchip (Wikipedia 2005a).

Now, 20 years on, dozens of the items in our home contain microchips, and life without the laptop, DVD player, mobile phone, Internet and MP3 player is unthinkable. Contrasting these two domestic situations, roughly 20 years apart, is indicative of the way microchips in devices have changed our lives. I am sure that in the future the microchip will continue to dominate and change the way we live our lives. I am also sure that 20 years ago I could not have imagined the way that the microchip has changed the way I live my life.

Returning to the sphere of education, as teachers, we might very well ask if this picture of progress and transformation through the microchip is also true of what is happening in schools.

To some extent we can say that the microchip in the form of Information and Communications Technology in the classroom has changed the way we teach and learn in schools, as much as it has changed the way we live our lives outside the sphere of education. But whether this change is fundamental is still very much an issue of debate. Despite an increasing body of evidence that ICT can have some positive effects on education (Harrison, Comber, *et al.* 2002) this is not really sufficient to make the case that ICT has transformed teaching and learning in our schools into something we couldn't imagine 20 years ago. In short, the impact of technology on education is not comparable to the impact of technology on life in general.

However, the question we must ask is, does this matter? To some extent it might be argued that it does, and that perhaps opportunities to learn in new and revolutionary ways have been squandered. On the other hand, it might be argued that the educational community's slightly sceptical and reserved attitude to technology has meant that the pace of progress has been steady but controlled. It might also be argued that the cost (measured in financial terms and in terms of teachers' time and effort) of trying to keep up with developments in technology in education would have been too great, and put too many other aspects of education at risk. Moreover, education is a very complex organisation and process and the introduction of ICT into this situation too quickly would be impossible because of the complexity.

To illuminate this point, consider the issue of video conferencing and the Internet. We know that this can and does work technologically via broadband Internet connections, yet it is used comparatively little in education, despite some interesting research having been done (Arnold, Cayley, *et al.* 2005). If we had taken this technology and used it to its full potential, we could have abolished schools altogether and teachers could communicate with groups and individuals via video, delivering teaching materials, perhaps through an Internet virtual learning environment. However, this hasn't happened, and for many good social, financial and pedagogical reasons. The end of the school as we know it does not seem at all likely!

However, technology enthusiasts, such as myself, might ask: Does it matter that we are not using technology to its full technological potential in our schools? Despite being a technological enthusiast and lifelong techie (since my first experiences in computer club in the 1980s), I would most assuredly say no. This is because I believe effective education is a complex balance of factors and situations. To allow it to be led simply by what technology can do would be a mistake and make light of the strong role of relationships, curriculum and social issues which form the fabric of education. *However*, technical issues are still a major factor in the success of ICT in schools, and as such they warrant a chapter in this book on ICT in schools. The reason for this is that technology is neither perfect nor universally reliable. Despite many improvements since the days of Sinclair home computing 20 years ago, teachers in the classroom, ICT subject leaders and school managers have to deal with technological problems every day.

This chapter is not about technology needing to develop more in order for it to be of benefit to education, it is about a much simpler issue – getting the technology used now to work.

Definition of terms

This glossary is not intended to be exhaustive, but can be used as a guide to support the technical discussion in this chapter and the book as a whole.

Hardware and devices

You might come across these terms in manuals or articles about computers.

Table 3.1 Hardware and devices

Purpose	Name	Definition
Types of computer	Desktop Computer	Computer which is designed to be kept in one place. Usually keyboard, mouse, hard drive box and monitor are separate components. The exception to this is the desktop Macintosh, the iMac, which has an integrated monitor and hard drive box. Runs on power from mains.
	Laptop Computer	Computer which is designed to be portable. Hard drive box, keyboard, monitor and mouse are integrated. Can run on battery or mains power.
	Tablet Computer	Computer which is designed to be portable and used by children. All elements are integrated into one flat device operated by tapping on the screen using the 'pen' which acts as a mouse.
Operating systems	Microsoft Windows Operating System	An operating system (OS) is a program which enables the computer to perform basic functions. The most common OS are versions of the Mircosoft Windows OS such as Windows 98 and Windows XP.
	Macintosh Operating System	Macintosh built computers run versions of the Macintosh Operating System, for example MacOS 10.
	UNIX Operating System	'Open source' (and therefore free to be adapted) operating system sometimes used on networks, although also available for stand alone machines. Such systems are considered 'free of charge' but users may need to pay for bundling, delivery and any subsequent technical support. The Linux OS also works along these lines.
Data collection	Datalogger	A variety of devices which collect data such as amounts of light heat or sound. Some devices are handheld and can be used independently of a computer, and others are wired up to a computer and produce results through software run on the computer.

Table 3.1 Hardware and devices (continued)

Purpose	Name	Definition
Image	Digital camera	Collects moving and still images and can be plugged directly into a printer or attached to a computer so images can be downloaded and manipulated.
	Electronic Microscope	Collects and displays magnified images and displays them on a computer.
	Scanner	Collects images from paper and converts them into digital form.
Paper document production	Printer	Creates paper copies of documents and files produced on the computer. Older dot-matrix versions have now been mostly replaced by ink-jet and laser printers.

Software types

Table 3.2 Software types

Purpose	Examples of Software	Example of Use
Word Processing	Word, Appleworks	Creating and manipulating text and image documents
Manipulating Images	Paint, Paintshop Pro, Appleworks, Adobe Photoshop, iPhoto	Creating and manipulating image documents, including scanned and photographs
Managing Data	Excel, Access, Appleworks	Creating spreadsheets and databases to manage, organise and interrogate data.
Presentation	PowerPoint	Creating slide shows including text, images and movies
Email	Outlook Express, Entourage, Eudora	Creating, sending and organising emails
Internet browser	Safari, Internet Explorer, Firefox	Displays web pages and other documents in HTML

You might come across these terms in manuals and when using different types of computer. The list is intended to show that there are many types of software which do similar things. In some cases, particularly when using Macintosh computers, you may get a choice of what to use, but in Windows there is usually only one program for each job. The most contentious of these is the Internet browser, where there are many options, some of which can be downloaded from the web and are 'open source' options.

File types

You will come across different file types in different kinds of programs. Each program will usually have a default file type, but you may save files in a variety of formats by choosing from the menu at the bottom of the 'save' dialogue box. Windows Operating System will automatically add a file extension to the file name you choose, so that if you share the file or reopen it from a folder the computer will know which program to use. This is also true of Macintosh Operating System X, although not older versions of MacOS.

Table 3.3 Types of file

Type of file	File extension (abbreviation at the end of the file)	Name of file
Word processing files	doc	Microsoft Word – word processing file
	dot	Microsoft Word – word processing template
	wps	Works text file – Old Mac word processing file
Text files	rtf	Rich Text Format – text format files which can retain some formatting when viewed in different word processing programs
	txt	Text file – a simple file for transferring unformatted text between different formats. Can be read by a wide variety of programs
	mcw	Macwrite text file – old Mac word processor text file
Spreadsheet files	xls	Excel file – Spreadsheet file created by Microsoft Excel
	wks	Works spreadsheet file – Mac created spreadsheet file
	csv	Comma separated variables – Comma delimited data file which can be created in spreadsheet programs

Table 3.3 Types of file (continued)

Type of file	File extension (abbreviation at the end of the file)	Name of file
PowerPoint files	ppt	PowerPoint file – presentation file created by Microsoft PowerPoint
	pot	PowerPoint template file – presentation template created by Microsoft PowerPoint
Internet files	html	Hypertext Mark-up Language file – standard format for web pages
	xml	Extensible Mark-up Language – enhanced web page format.
Email file	eml	Microsoft email file
Image file	jpeg	Joint Photographic Expert Group file – common file type for images on the web. Images using 256 colours are compressed and stored in relatively small files.
	gif	Graphical Interchange format – common file type for images on the web. New types of gif files can simulate animation by storing several images.
	tif	Tagged Image File format – common file type for images on the web
	bmp	Bitmap file – common format for image files created by drawing programs. Creates large file sizes in comparison to jpeg
	png	Portable network graphics file – similar to gif file but the compression system is in the public domain, as opposed to the new gif format which is silenced
Moving image files	wmf	Windows Media file – standard format for moving images created by Microsoft software
	mov	Movie file – Standard movie format read by QuickTime
	mpeg	Moving Pictures Expert Group – compressed video file
Music files	wav	Windows Audio File – standard format for audio files created by Microsoft windows
	wma	Windows Media Audio – the Microsoft alternative to the dominant MP3 file type
	mp3	Mpeg audio layer 3 file – compressed sound file made popular by downloadable music
	aac	Advanced Audio Coding – standard Mac format audio file

Connectivity and bandwidth

Table 3.4 Connectivity and bandwidth

Term	Abbreviation	Definition
Network		Collection of computers which are connected together
Local area network	LAN	A collection of computers collected together, typically in one company or school
Connectivity	–	The type of connection a computer has to its network
World wide web	www	One part of the Internet where communication takes place. The Internet is bigger than the www, which is why some URLs don't start with www (for example news.bbc.co.uk).
Bandwidth	–	The rate at which a system allows computers on that network to communicate with one another. The 'wider' the bandwidth, the faster the communication.
Protocol	–	The way in which computers communicate – computers on the same network need to be able to use the same protocols to communicate
Packet		An amount of information transferred over a network
Uniform resource locator	URL	An address on the Internet which is unique to that resource. These are usually defined by numbers, although we see them as words in the address bar on the browser.
HyperText transfer protocol	http	The most common communication protocol over the Internet. That's why web pages start with http://, whether they are on the www or not.
File transfer protocol	ftp	An alternative protocol for transferring files over the Internet
Broadband	–	Fast connection to a network. The speed is undefined officially, but it is a faster connection than is available over a conventional telephone line.
Modulator/ demodulator	Modem	The part of a computer which links between the network and the computer itself. In the early days these were external devices but now most new computers come with one of these built in.
Integrated services digital network	ISDN	A type of digital connection to a network, as Distinct from an old analog phone line
Digital subscriber line	DSL	These can either be synchronous, or asynchronous. A synchronous DSL (ADSL) will have the same upload and download speed.

The Internet

Table 3.5 The Internet

Term	Definition
Blog	Short for weblog – freely available web space where individuals or organisations can publish thoughts and ideas
Bookmarks/ Favourites	Links to Internet pages which are saved by your browser.
Browser	Displays web pages and other documents in html. Functions on the tool bar also help navigate the Internet.
Cache	A store of web pages on a local server which saves the system from having to go back out onto the Internet to access frequently used pages. The impact should be that access to web pages is faster.
Cookie	A file sent to your computer by a website which enables you to access the website more easily next time. A cookie for example, could enable you to log on using a saved username and password.
Domain	First part of a web address (URL)
Refresh button	Button on your web browser which asks for the version of the webpage you are looking at to be updated from the source.
Frames	Some web pages contain several areas which operate independently of one another. These are called frames. This might allow a message board, for instance to always display a list of users while the messages scroll down as they are added.
Internet	The global network which links computers and allows them to communicate using a range of protocols.
IP address	The specific address of a computer on the network/Internet
Plug in	An extra program which allows a user to access a game or animation over the Internet. This is complementary to the Internet browser.
World wide web	A part of the Internet. Addresses for all web pages which are part of this are prefixed by www.
Web page	A single 'page' of html/xml coded information which appears over the Internet.

The development of the computer and the Internet

When Charles Babbage invented his 'difference engine' (a machine for calculations) in the 1820s he surely cannot have imagined how machines would develop from these initial ideas into modern computers, although many would argue that his invention was the first 'computer'. By the mid-1950s companies and inventors were using machines to help with calculations, however these machines, although complex, were still mechanical rather than using the technology we use today in computers. The revolution in technology came when Robert Noyce, a Massachusetts Institute of Technology graduate and Jack Kirlby, who filed the first patent for an integrated circuit or microchip in 1959, began to manufacture their semiconductors from silicon. They sold these to international business machines who began to use them in calculating machines. In the late 1960s Intel was formed by Noyce, and the age of the computer, built using microprocessors, had begun.

In the 1970s three computer enthusiasts based in California set up their own business building computers. Initially their machines were sold only to specialists, but in 1977 the Apple II took the business computer market – where Commodore and Tandy were also players – by storm. It was this year that Ken Olsen, founder of the Digital Equipment Corporation, said that there was no reason anyone would want a computer in their home. History does not record whether he thought anyone would want one in their school, but by the 1980s schools were indeed beginning to use computers, such as the BBC Micro, built by Acorn computers, in classrooms to run simple educational programs. By the early 1990s the inception of the National Curriculum enshrined the place of ICT in schools and Apple Mac and the new personal computers (PCs) running Intel microprocessors began to compete for a slice of the lucrative educational market place (Wikipedia 2005b).

The pace of computer developments in education

The beginning of the story of the computer has its fair share of creative geniuses, competition and acrimony. Nearly 50 years on, intense rivalry between Apple Macintosh and Intel/Microsoft is still one of the main drivers of progress and innovation in the computer industry. But rivalry has also been the source of problems. Most teachers and schools just want computer equipment that will work and be useful to them in teaching and learning. But the pace of progress and compatibility issues have often meant that equipment in schools has sometimes been unreliable, and has quickly become incompatible or obsolete.

Nearly 20 years since the first computers reached the classroom, the pace of technological developments continues to outstrip the pace of pedagogical developments. This could be seen as a substantial barrier to teaching and learning with ICT. However, with schools and LEAs increasingly planning procurement carefully, and as compatibility of new technologies with old becomes easier, it may be that schools actually begin to choose and dictate which technologies they use. The range and diversity of technologies now can support innovation and developments have made computers more reliable and affordable than ever.

Considering all these technological developments, however, it is not enough to make ICT successfully achieve its potential in teaching and learning in schools. ICT must win over the 'hearts and minds' of the teaching profession too (Wheeler 2005). In order to do this technical barriers need to be overcome to enable teachers to get the best of the available technology without having to wonder if the technology will actually work.

Technical barriers to successful ICT in schools: A summary

Software and operating systems

The majority of schools in the UK use the computers which are PCs, although some do use the Apple Macintosh platform. The majority of the PCs use the Microsoft Windows Operating System. There are few problems with the XP version, but some schools have had problems with Windows NT, as adding new and non-Microsoft software can be difficult. Those running Macintosh operating systems may have found that some educational software will not work with MacOS. The solution to these problems might lie in using UNIX operating systems, but with technical support limited for many UNIX operating systems, this might be difficult for schools without sufficient technical expertise and time.

Software has become increasingly reliable. As computers have become more powerful, old problems where programs 'freeze' or 'crash' have been minimised. However there are still some issues of compatibility, particularly between specialist educational software and proprietary applications such as Microsoft Office. For instance the popular primary school word processor Textease creates files which can only be read by this software, so can't be opened in Microsoft Word. This is similar to the problems many Apple Mac users encountered when using ClarisWorks before most educational Mac users were able to get Microsoft Office for MacOS. (Table 3.2, above, lists many common file types.) The range and diversity of file types, performing different functions, continues to increase, however operating systems are now largely designed to enable a suitable program to open the file to be found automatically.

Bandwidth and the Internet

During the first phase of the development of connectivity (known as the National Grid for Learning project, see Chapter 2) most schools were connected to the Internet via a DSL. This meant that larger schools, especially secondaries, had some significant problems with speed of access. Even with good provision for caching, access was often still not at a speed which meant the Internet could be used in lessons. Most schools are now connected to the broadband network, which has solved this problem to some extent. However, the Regional Broadband Consortia (RBC) are developing a range of resources to be used over the broadband network which need substantial bandwidth, such as video. With the development of such resources it is likely that schools and LEAs must plan to increase bandwidth further.

The Internet is ever-growing. Every day more pages are added and more information is available to teachers and learners. However quantity is by no means a guarantee of quality. Therefore teachers must teach pupils to use the information they find on the Internet with caution, and which sites are more likely to be reliable.

Personal safety and the Internet

A small number of high-profile cases have led teachers, schools and parents to question whether it is safe for children to use the Internet. There is understandable concern about the types of information available on the web which may not be suitable for children to view. In addition, some parents and teachers might think that communication via email, chat rooms and message boards may put children at risk.

However, I would argue that these concerns are not a good reason to stop children using the Internet in their learning. The possible benefits of using the Internet to support research and learning outweigh the risks. In addition, the Internet plays such a central role in our society that it seems to be much more sensible to teach children to use the Internet safely and responsibly.

Most LEAs filter the Internet service to schools. This is designed to block any unsuitable content. However what some schools consider unsuitable might be useful to others, which raises difficulties for those responsible for blocking content. In addition most schools also have an 'acceptable use' policy for using the Internet, which sets out expectations and rules for use.

Overcoming barriers and identifying benefits

Twenty-first-century schools are places where policies, development plans, audits and other paperwork are commonplace. Some teachers and school managers might question the effectiveness of these documents on helping the school to progress. However, in the context of ICT, forward planning is essential if some technical barriers are to be overcome. Schools and LEAs need to have plans for technical development.

The first set of barriers exists around computer operating systems and software. Compatibility problems have decreased as software and operating systems have become more sophisticated, but schools and LEAs still need to plan carefully. Running a combination of Apple Macintosh computers and PCs on the same network is possible, but can be problematic. Where possible it is simpler to choose one type of computer and one operating system. Therefore when planning a replacement strategy for computer equipment within schools, it is essential to plan for maximum compatibility.

Despite the fact that most schools are now connected to broadband, schools will still need to deal with the issues around getting fast and reliable access to Internet-based resources. To some extent, caching would support this, but with increasing use of images, audio and video over websites and virtual learning environments, schools will still need to consider whether the access to these resources is fast enough to teach with them effectively. It is therefore likely that in future planning schools should consider how to budget to maintain and increase bandwidth.

The Internet is a vast and easily accessible source of information for all ages. Unfortunately, it is almost entirely unregulated, and consequently is also a potential source of inaccurate information. In addition, the Internet is also used to publish material which is not suitable for children. The challenge for schools is to make the best of the potential of the Internet while avoiding misleading or inappropriate information. This can be done both at a technical and pedagogical level. Schools and LEAs employ sophisticated filters on their Internet access, which to a large extent, block out any inappropriate content both in terms of text and images. These systems are backed up by the ability of teachers to report any inappropriate material to the filter provider, and for sites to be blocked accordingly. These types of systems are backed up with school 'acceptable use' policies, which require pupils to be aware of the rules and use the Internet safely and responsibly. The content of this policy is dependent on the age of the children, the kind of access they are given, and the type of school. However common elements might include:

- what the Internet and email can be used for – schools usually limit this by saying that school connections can only be used for purposes which relate to school work;
- when the Internet can be used – some schools limit this to time when a teacher or other member of staff is present;
- basic principles of safety on the Internet, for instance telling children never to give out real names, or any contact details;
- ensuring children understand how to report to an adult anything which they don't like or makes them feel uncomfortable.

In addition to teaching children how to use the Internet safely, teachers also need to instruct children on how to sift through and use information from the Internet. It is important to teach children, right from the first time they use the Internet, to treat what the read and see thoughtfully. There are some Internet sites which are very 'reliable', for example, the BBC (www.bbc.co.uk), but there are many others which could be turned up by search engines which are not. However there are also some websites which are editable by their users and so are 'open' about the sources of their information. Probably the best of these is Wikipedia (http://en.wikipedia.org) which contains a wide range of information which readers can add to. Sites like this teach children that the Internet is not just a static source of information, but a way of sharing and communicating information.

Safe and appropriate use of the Internet and policies and procedures which support this are the responsibility of LEAs, schools and individual teachers. In the relationships between these three stakeholders, there is a balance to be struck between establishing a framework which supports the policies and procedures, but also gives some freedom to allow schools or even teachers to access what they consider appropriate and useful content. Therefore communication about how the Internet can be used must be at the centre of establishing a system which works for all.

Expert help

Most schools and teachers are supported technically and in terms of pedagogy by in-house support staff or by LEA-based technicians and courses. However, increasingly, teachers need to find quick and easy solutions to technical and pedagogical problems, as well as some new ideas for teaching and learning opportunities.

Technical help

- Most programs contain a 'help' button on the top toolbar, which provides support in finding out how to operate the software.
- Websites can provide useful support, especially in the area of 'frequently asked questions' (FAQs). Most large software providers such as Blackcat have useful sites such as http://www.blackcatsoftware.com/help/help.asp.
- For problems with Microsoft software or operating systems a wide range of 'troubleshooting tips' are available online http://support.microsoft.com/gp/hublist.
- Similar support for Apple Mac hardware, operating systems and software http://www.apple.com/support/.

Pedagogical support

- BECTA provides a range of online and downloadable advice about ICT pedagogy, both in terms of general issues such as personalising learning and in terms of specific issues, such as what research says about the use of interactive whiteboards: http://www.becta.org.uk/.
- Nesta Futurelab also publishes advice and literature reviews on issues connected with the pedagogy of ICT in schools: http://www.nestafuturelab.org/.
- Examples of children's work, linked in with the National Curriculum and established assessment strategies, are available at http://www.ncaction.org.uk/subjects/ict/inother.htm.
- Creative use of ICT is promoted at http://www.ncaction.org.uk/creativity/index.htm.

Help with innovation and imaginative ideas

- Free software including a typing tutor is available at http://www.kiranreddys.com/index.html.
- Publish and share ideas on the online editable encyclopaedia Wikipedia: http://en.wikipedia.org/wiki/Main_Page.
- Start Blogging: http://www.blogger.com/start.

Policy and practice for safe use of ICT

Schools must ensure that they have adequate filtering and security systems to protect their schools and ICT users from unwanted information and dangerous computer viruses. However, there are also some steps which schools need to take to ensure that the users of ICT do not put themselves and the systems at risk.

An 'Acceptable Use' agreement is important in a school. It helps staff and pupils understand how to protect themselves, other users and the school's hardware and software from risk. This agreement might be signed by staff, pupils and/or their parents.

A good review of the issues which should help teachers develop an agreement are available from the NSPCC at: http://www.nspcc.org.uk/html/Home/Needadvice/surfingsafelytipsforyoungpeople.htm.

References

Arnold, T., Cayley, S., Griffith, M. (2005) *Video Conferencing in the Classroom*. BECTA, Coventry.

Harrison, C., Comber, C., Fisher, T., Haw, K., Lewin, C., Luzner, E., McFarlane, A., Mavers, D., Scrimshaw,

P., Somekh, B., Watling, R. (2002) *ImpaCT2: The Impact of Information and Communication on Pupil Learning and Attainment. Strand 1 Report.* DfES, London.

Wheeler, S. (2005) *Transforming Primary ICT.* Learning Matters, Exeter.

Wikipedia (2005a) Wikipedia, the free encyclopedia: http://en.wikipedia.org/wiki/Main_Page.

Wikipedia (2005b) Wikipedia, the free encyclopedia, computing timeline: http://en.wikipedia.org/wiki/Computing_timeline.

CHAPTER 4

Training teachers to use learning technology

Background and introduction

> By learning you will teach, by teaching you will learn.
>
> (Latin proverb)

The relationship between teaching and learning may seem to some to be an obvious one, with the two actions being inextricably linked. Yet the issue of whether in practice teachers always make good learners remains a controversial one. Anyone who has (like me) worked in initial teacher training and in providing continuing professional development for teachers will know that a wide range of factors affect whether the group of professionals we call 'teachers' are effective 'learners'. The aim of this chapter is to examine what, in the context if ICT in the classroom, these factors are.

It may be that to unlock the barriers to developing an effective learning culture in the teaching profession, the history of training and professional development needs to be examined. Teachers who are currently approaching retirement trained in colleges have, during their career, had mixed access to professional development. In contrast to this, most new teachers have trained through the higher education route, and their career path and professional development opportunities have been carefully planned and structured.

Jill's experience in teacher training college in the 1960s

In the 1950s and 1960s the majority of teachers in primary schools and many in secondary schools (except for academic subjects in grammar schools) were drawn from the Teacher Training colleges – further education colleges devoted entirely to the one vocational course. The courses beginning in the early 1960s were three years long, having just been changed from a two-year course, and some students had the impression that the three-year course had not really been thought out thoroughly at that time, and that the three-year course was essentially the same as the two-year course. This meant student training was busy but not intense.

The curriculum was widely based and Jill was expected to study many subjects: a main subject and a second subject, to be chosen from the normal range of subjects: History, Geography, Maths, Needlework, Woodwork, English or Art. It wasn't until the late 1980s that ICT was introduced into the teacher training curriculum. Trainees handwrote and presented their essays, plans and assessments. There was pressure put on students to produce the best work they could, ensuring that the work was beautifully presented, illustrations and maps had to be at least double-mounted and there were no computer graphics to help – it all had to be all done by hand.

Teaching practice meant Jill, who was studying to teach at junior level, spent two days in infant school, three days in senior school and two weeks in junior. The second teaching placement took place over four weeks, and the students knew that at any time their tutors could turn up and observe them. In the third year there was a ten-week practice, with weekly visits from tutors. Teaching jobs were relatively easy to come by, although some of Jill's fellow students were told where they were going to be offered a particular post rather than having much choice.

As these teachers progressed through their careers in the 1970s and 1980s, opportunities for continuing professional development were sporadic. Although many went on into school management there were no formal structures or requirements for this. As far as the introduction of learning technology into schools goes, during the 1980s, BBC computers began to be most used, provided that schools could afford them, as computers were funded out of general school funds, which were pressurised during the later 1970s and throughout the 1980s. Jill found that there were a few really good programs to use and time on the computer had to be rationed so that all the children in the class could have a 'turn'. With only one computer in school, the computer would be on a trolley and wheeled from class to class.

Gradually through the latter half of the 1980s, computer rooms we set up so that classes had timetabled slots, usually once a week, ensuring pupils had access to ICT. In the late 1980s and early 1990s, changes in the teaching profession were brought about by the inception of the National Curriculum, which gave a new impetus to professional development. Around this time, PCs arrived and computing, instead of being just a technical subject where children learnt computing skills, became a tool for teachers and pupils to access and impart information over the whole curriculum.

Catherine's experiences of teacher training in the year 2000

Having completed a three-year BA in History of Art, Catherine did a one-year PGCE specialising in the lower primary age range. Before this she worked for a year as a teaching assistant in an infant school. Many entrants to the teaching profession in the twenty-first century have similar experiences, having first taken a relevant degree either in a curriculum subject or in a related subject such as psychology, and then done a postgraduate teaching qualification. In addition many entrants to the profession have worked in education in other capacities. During the first term Catherine had one short teaching practice of three weeks, in which she was paired with another trainee.

Generally students (or trainees as they were now known) were paired with different specialists – and often with different personalities. During this practice and the next they are assessed on their ability to 'Team Teach' – work together in teaching, planning and assessing, and special focus is given to their reviewing of each other. This was good preparation for the increasing collaborative nature of the teachers' role. The final summer term practice, the longest, was completed individually. During this, trainees taught independently most days, wrote some reports, took a full role in marking, assessing and even in things like school plays.

Between practices Catherine and her fellow trainees had to fit what used to be done in three years into approximately five months of taught time in the higher education institution. The curriculum was largely based around the National Curriculum and professional studies. Training in ICT was extensive and covered PowerPoint, digital video, camera and tape recording. With the relatively new addition of the literacy, numeracy and ICT skills tests these three subjects were a particular focus.

Teacher training – some conclusions

Both of these groups (and many teachers whose experience falls somewhere between these two scenarios) work together in schools today. Designing an ICT training and Continuing Professional Development (CPD) programme which meets needs as diverse as these presents many difficulties. To summarise the main differences:

- The three-year route allowed for time to reflect and the development of students' own interests. The nine-month postgraduate route has far less time for this kind of personal development. Therefore expectations of CPD may differ, as may approaches to the formality of CPD.

- Recently trained teachers have had comprehensive training in using ICT, whereas other teachers have generally learned what they know while serving as teachers. This means levels of confidence and competence vary enormously between colleagues in the same school.

- The focus on collaboration in more recent teacher training programmes prepares more recently trained teachers for the collaborative nature of CPD, where teachers exchange ideas and support one another's professional development. Teachers of all ages and experiences work well like this, but the culture of the autonomy for the teacher in their own classroom is one which is no longer prevalent.

New opportunities fund ICT training

This gives a context to ICT professional development initiatives. During the first phase of development in the NGfL initiative (see Chapter 2) teachers were offered training and professional development which were funded through the National Lottery's New Opportunities Fund (NOF) (DfES 2005). Reflecting on this scheme the Teachernet website acknowledges that this was only intended to be 'basic' and that more development was needed. The NOF scheme did at least mean that some training relating to pedagogy with ICT was available to all serving teachers and before it a combination of LEA and independently provided courses meant that access to training was dependent on the school funds and the teacher's situation. However, the impact of the scheme has been widely criticised (TES 2005). Extensive studies which have been conducted into the impact of the training initiative (Preston 2004; Client 2005) back up this criticism to some extent, although a final qualitative analysis of the results of the initiative are positive (Preston 2004).

Essentially, the NOF funded training aimed to provide some phase and subject-specific ICT training for teachers and librarians in schools. This training was delivered via a range of 'Approved Training Providers', whom it was hoped, would develop a range of programmes to suit a wide variety of needs in schools. The training providers, some small and regional, others large and prestigious organisations, did indeed offer diversity. However the speed with which the initiative was rushed into schools, along with the fact that this was the first attempt at training of the teaching workforce on this scale, meant that some fundamental mistakes were made. Crucially the intention that teachers would receive some technical training before the programme began was not realised, and so teachers with vastly different technical ability to use IT attempted to follow the same training programme. Reflecting on the differences in initial and continuing professional training of the workforce outlined in the introduction, this was obviously problematic. In addition the 'roll out' of NGfL funding meant that some schools or individuals did not have the necessary hardware, software or connectivity necessary to carry out the programmes of training effectively.

However, given all these barriers, the Mirandanet evaluation of the effectiveness of the programme reports that three quarters of teachers who responded to their questionnaire reported successful learning of one kind or another occurred as a result of the initiative (Preston 2004).

In essence what was learned from the NOF training programme was that:

- ICT skills need development alongside pedagogical skills in using ICT.
- Teachers need different programmes of development depending on their skills, situation and interests.
- Equipment needs to be in place before teachers are trained in its use.
- The majority of teachers' professional development benefited from the opportunity to improve their ICT and pedagogical skills in this way.

Teacher education, training and development and ICT

To some extent it may be argued that trends in teacher education, training and development (even to the extent of what we call the practice of educating teachers) is defined by the educational values which are current. In essence both initial teacher training (ITT) and continuing professional development (CPD), as I shall call them, reflect the values of the system in which those teachers work in their nature, content, curriculum and modes of delivery.

Buzz words in education currently might include 'personalised learning', 'differing learning styles' and 'assessment'. As these issues are forced onto the agenda of teachers in schools in relation to the education of their pupils, they also become current issues in teacher education, training and development. Yet the interplay between values in these two contexts is more complex than it first appears. Robin Alexander (Soler, Craft, *et al.* 2001) calls this value system a culture, and asserts that the pedagogy of a culture is a reflection of that culture. He defines pedagogy as 'a purposeful mix of educational values and principles in action of planning content strategy and technique, of learning and assessment and of relationships both instrumental and affective' (Soler, Craft *et al.* 2001). Considering this idea in relation to current cultures in ITE and CPD, I would characterise the culture, and therefore the pedagogy thus:

- Initial teacher training is defined by a set of standards and requirements. Essentially it is a competency-based approach, which requires providers to give trainee teachers the opportunity and support to prove their competence in the defined standards. In addition trainees must pass some standard tests, including one in ICT skills, in order to gain qualified teacher status (QTS).

- Continuing Professional Development is now inextricably linked with promotion and pay levels for teachers. Teachers' pay scales now only allow progression if teachers can demonstrate both competency in their work and a willingness to continue to engage in professional development.

In both these systems there is little emphasis on the link between professional and personal development, the age-old value of education having some intrinsic worth to the individual. With this in mind, I shall now examine the status quo of ITE and CPD specifically in relation to ICT and seek to define what might make training in this context effective.

Initial teacher training and ICT

Standards and requirements for ICT training in initial teacher training

The requirements for initial teacher training providers are set out by the Teacher Training Agency:

> Requirement 4.2 – All providers must ensure that trainee teachers have access to the books, ICT and other resources they need – relevant to the age ranges and subjects they are training for – to develop trainee teachers' knowledge, understanding and skills to at least the Standards required for the award of Qualified Teacher Status.
>
> (TTA 2003a)

In the further guidance, the use of ICT to disseminate materials electronically is also encouraged.

This standard is general in nature, and provision differs widely among providers. Some higher education institutions might provide a range of tools, including computer suites, whiteboards and portable devices. Trainees undertaking school-based routes via the Graduate Training Programme will have access to what the school are about to provide. Therefore experiences will differ very widely, and crucially, the extent to which providers who are able to model good practice through their own use of ICT will be heavily dependent on their own resources.

The standards for Initial Teacher Training are intended to bring some common criteria to the range of ITE. They apply not only to all phases, but also to all routes for training from purely vocational school-based training to those studying for higher degrees which encompass Qualified Teacher Status (QTS).

There are two standards which relate directly to ICT:

> Standard 2.5 – Those awarded Qualified Teacher Status must demonstrate that they know how to use ICT effectively, both to teach their subject and to support their wider professional role.
>
> (TTA 2003a)

Standard 3.3.10 – Those awarded Qualified Teacher Status must demonstrate that they use ICT effectively in their teaching.

(TTA 2003a)

ICT is also alluded to in standards on resources and subject knowledge. These standards can be effectively addressed in a taught ITT programme, where course tutors incorporate ICT into each subject, in addition to the trainees working on specific ICT skills.

The manifestation of these skills and requirements in a trainee's practice differs significantly depending on the phase of training, as well as on the type of training being undertaken. In a best practice scenario, trainees will be able to apply ICT constructively in their teaching, where ICT will support learning and enhance teaching. For a foundation stage trainee this might mean pupils using a digital camera to take pictures for a class book; for a key stage 2 trainee, this might mean using data logging equipment to measure temperature in a science experiment. At key stage 4 trainees might set pupils a 'web quest' in search of information about a historical event. In each of these examples the trainee will use ICT confidently.

In practice, though, a trainee's ability to *apply* ICT effectively in their teaching depends upon the schools in which they undertake their practical teaching experience. Particularly in the primary sector, where the size of schools and available resources differ greatly, experiences in teaching practice can vary enormously and have a substantial influence on a trainee's confidence and competence in using ICT in their teaching.

The ICT skills test

In addition to the ICT element of Initial Teacher Training, all trainees must pass skills tests in English, Mathematics and ICT in order to gain Qualified Teacher Status. These tests are additional to the assessment procedures of the ITT course. The aims for the test are set out on the TTA website:

> The QTS skills test in Information and Communications Technology (ICT) is intended to ensure that everyone qualifying to teach has a good grounding in the use of ICT in the wider context of their professional role as a teacher. The ICT skills tested are relevant to all teachers and do not assess the broader range of ICT knowledge that is required by those training to teach ICT. Neither do the tests assess the range of knowledge required by the ICT Initial Teacher Training (ITT) National Curriculum which sets out what teachers need in order to use ICT effectively in teaching their subjects. ITT providers assess these broader ranges of knowledge as part of their ITT programmes.

(TTA 2005)

To say that these tests have proved to be a controversial issue for trainee teachers is an understatement. Discussions among trainee teachers on forums such as the TES messageboards show that trainees find the tests stressful. However, most trainees have no difficulties in passing the tests if they prepare themselves using the practice tests or some of the practice books available. In addition those who teach ICT in ITE question whether the tests in their current format do 'ensure that everyone qualifying to teach has a good grounding in the use of ICT'. Trainees are required to undertake a range of tasks in the following types of software:

- word processing
- spreadsheet
- database
- presentation
- email
- browser.

The versions used in the test are simulated 'generic' software types.

As a result of this, and the ways in which the tests are designed, many trainees have encountered the following problems:

- The test environment does not allow trainees to employ their usual techniques for using software such as keyboard shortcuts or right button clicks.
- The tasks have to be completed in a way which the simulation requires, rather than any creative/imaginative approach a trainee might want to use.
- Trainees are allowed 35 minutes to complete the test, which puts them under additional time pressure which is not realistic.
- The test does not aim to help trainees with ICT use in the classroom, and the skills learned in order to pass the test are largely not transferable to the classroom environment.

It seems unlikely that the tests will be withdrawn since they are enshrined in the standards for the award of QTS (standard 2.8). However, they are likely to remain a controversial issue with trainees and ITE tutors for both practical and philosophical reasons.

Case study research into ICT in ITE

A number of ITE tutors have worked on small-scale research projects into the effect of ICT in ITE. Recently the Teacher Training Agency has begun to fund such projects, and the hope is that this funding will continue to enable tutors to develop their own (and through publication the ITE community's) understanding of how the development of ICT as a pedagogical tool and a resources for the classroom impacts trainees' professional development.

One small-scale study was completed in the faculty of education at the University of Cambridge (Taylor 2004). The aim was to examine what student teachers make of ICT and how changing understanding of its role throughout the course impacts trainees' skills in using ICT in the classroom. Taylor sets out a three-stage model of the development of the trainees:

- Stage 1 – Process of personalisation
- Stage 2 – Growth in pedagogical sensitivity
- Stage 3 – Development of contingent thinking.

In her study, Taylor followed a cohort of secondary-phase Geography trainee teachers over the course of their PGCE. The study came to some illuminating conclusions, and offers some implications for ICT in ITE. First, she explains, ICT learning needs to be planned with trainee teachers' learning needs in mind as well as the desirable end product of the skills and knowledge they need to take from the course into their NQT year. Second, there are some aspects of ICT skills and knowledge which develop sooner than others; for instance, in that particular cohort, the trainees grasped the issues related to ICT and behaviour management quicker than they were able to plan for effective differentiation of both subject knowledge and ICT skills in one activity. Unsurprisingly, Taylor also found there was a relationship between trainees' personal ICT skills and their ability to gain pedagogical knowledge in ICT. Finally, the extent to which ICT skills and pedagogy should be separate from other pedagogical skills also proved an issue. These issues, although raised in this small-scale context, are crucial for the future development of ICT in ITE.

OfSTED's characteristics of very good training, while not referring in particular to these issues in relation to ICT do back up Taylor's findings. The characteristics state that:

> Though the training is very well structured it is not inflexible, and trainers are sensitive to, and meet, the needs of individual trainees.
>
> (OfSTED 2002)

This backs up Taylor's findings which indicate that successful Initial Teacher Training needs to be flexible in terms of content and of its response to trainees' individual needs. This theme is further discussed below in the definition of what teachers want from ICT training.

Although the ICT aspect of ITT may form the basis of a teacher's understanding of ICT pedagogy, without good-quality Continuing Professional Development (CPD) the gains made during time spent in ITE will quickly be lost.

Continuing professional development and ICT

Earlier in the chapter, a teacher trained in the 1960s, Joan, told us that in the early 1990s PCs began to be introduced into schools, along with the new expectations of teaching and learning related to the National Curriculum. She reflects on the professional development at this stage:

> When PCs came into school, teachers demanded training as it was felt that it was ridiculous to be expected to teach all the new skills without fully understanding the amazing range of facilities the PC offered in comparison to the dear old BBC. Either teachers went out to courses or in the case of my school, we had an expert come in and we had to attend a series of twilight lessons to give us a basic understanding.

This effectively characterises the professional development of many teachers – twilight sessions given by an 'expert' (in this case an expert in computing rather than in the use of computing in teaching and learning). In addition, Joan was lucky enough to continue her professional development, albeit in her 'own' time:

> After that, we as a staff had to complete, in our own time, four modules, proving levels of competence in word processing, spreadsheets, databases and graphics.

Many teachers would not have received such support.

The contrast of this with Catherine's experiences on her ITE course is stark:

> Training in ICT was extensive and covered PowerPoint, digital video, camera and tape recording.

However in the early years of the twenty-first century, both Catherine and Joan were facing the challenge of keeping their skills up to date sufficiently to use it in their teaching. The issues of the NOF-funded ICT training have been discussed, and the lessons learned are restated below:

- ICT skills need development alongside pedagogical skills in using ICT.
- Teachers need different programmes of development depending on their skills, situation and interests.
- Equipment needs to be in place before teachers are trained in its use.
- The majority of teachers' professional development benefited in some way from the opportunity to improve their ICT and pedagogical skills in this way.

These lessons have had a direct impact on the next phase of ICT training in schools, the Hands on Support Initiative.

Hands on support

The Hands on Support (HOS)... is a new programme of peer to peer support for teachers, aimed at providing them with face to face support in their own classroom environment in the effective use of ICT in teaching and learning.

(DfES 2004c)

The principal aim of the Hands on Support initiative is clear in this DfES report: teachers can expect direct help with ICT which is relevant and delivered in a face to face manner. Schools and LEAs have worked together to devise a suitable programme of training which works within one of the following models:

- Model 1 – Central HOS programme designed, managed and delivered by the LEA
- Model 2 – Buy-in HOS programme – schools work in clusters to purchase a service
- Model 3 – Buy-in HOS programme – individual schools purchase a service
- Model 4 – HOS programme managed and delivered within an individual school.

(DfES 2004c)

The majority of LEAs have schools which have either chosen Model 1, where the programme is centrally delivered by the LEA; or Model 3, where the school have chosen to be autonomous and find their own solutions (these might be from within the school's expertise, from an independent company or other similar source). A significant number of LEAs have schools which have chosen from more than one model, which might be according to the phase or type of school.

At the time of writing, information on initiative was sparse. However it was possible to find evidence that the initiative was closely linked to the current pedagogical developments in training through the Primary Strategy, key stage 3 strategy and 14–19 project (DfES 2005). Therefore the Hands on Support should be closely linked to other professional development initiatives, which connect to the strategies and 14–19 project. OfSTED have found that effective ICT teaching is most often well-linked with effective teaching within other subjects (OfSTED 2004a; OfSTED 2004b) and thus the decision to link this training initiative with other CPD and school development seems sensible.

The crucial question about the initiative is whether it will provide the type and quality of training to meet schools' needs. This may, to a large extent, be governed by the initiative's ability to address the needs of individual teachers, whether their experience reflects Joan's above, or is closer to Catherine's. In the guidance for providers, the criteria for quality assurance are set out in detail:

Quality means a degree of excellence; assurance means a formal guarantee or positive declaration. Providers should be able to guarantee that they will consistently deliver high quality support. Quality assurance systems put in place procedures and processes that monitor and evaluate effectiveness in a realistic and practical way. All HOS providers will need to consider how to quality assure their HOS provision to ensure each of the following:

- The quality and usefulness of the support provided to the teacher;
- The increase in teachers' confidence to use ICT in teaching and learning; and
- The increase in teachers' recognition of how ICT is helping them to teach more effectively.

(DfES 2004c)

Unfortunately the DfES is still in the early stages of evaluating the project so there is little data to compare to the findings from the evaluation of the NOF-funded training, and it is difficult to assess the success of training overall.

Given this, I remain optimistic that the Hands on Support initiative will prove more successful than NOF. This is further supported in looking at another small-scale study, this time conducted into CPD (known in this case as staff development).

McCartney conducted a survey among serving teachers in Scotland (McCartney 2002) which examined their preferences for modes of professional development. Considering these in the context of the findings of the Mirandanet evaluation of the NOF-funded initiative it is possible to draw out that teachers, on the whole, value face-to-face interaction in CPD rather than distance learning models. In addition McCartney found that teachers needed not only technical training but also support with pedagogical development in using ICT. Despite the small-scale and specific nature of this study, there are themes emerging which can be seen in other projects.

The laptops for teachers scheme

In Spring 2002 the government launched the laptops for teachers scheme, aimed at increasing access to computers for teachers to use in both their teaching and wider professional role. This followed several schemes over the past few years where portable computers have been made available to school staff. After the first year the DfES commissioned a study into the outcomes of the scheme. This study (Cunningham, Kerr, et al. 2003) aimed to evaluate the scheme in seven key areas of teacher confidence and competence with computers:

- Assess the impact of laptop ownership on recipients' teaching and administration practices and use of resources.
- Assess the impact of laptop ownership on recipients' ICT competence, confidence and motivation.

- Explore recipients' perceptions of the value of ICT in teaching and learning.
- Assess the impact of laptop ownership on student motivation and attainment.
- Assess the impact of the laptops on teacher workload and that of other staff in the school.
- Assess the impact of portability including the benefits and issues related to security, health and safety and insurance.
- Assess the impact on communication and sharing of information with colleagues, students, parents, governors and others inside and outside school.

Key findings of the evaluation included increased teacher confidence and motivation in using computers in teaching. Also, crucially, many teachers surveyed said that having a laptop motivated them to extend their knowledge and skills in using ICT. In addition the scheme has proved beneficial in developing communication networks around school, which can only serve to benefit CPD. In the Mirandanet evaluation of the NOF-funded training, teachers being unable to access the appropriate technology was cited as one of the problems with the training. Provision of laptops through this scheme should support future training initiatives.

The role of ICT specialists in training

Many schools are lucky enough to have at least one ICT specialist, someone who is interested in and motivated by ICT, and has some special skills. OfSTED have found that in both primary and secondary sectors, this specialist is a defining factor in the success of ICT teaching and learning in a school. They also found that where teachers were able to share good practice, this also had a positive impact on the effective embedding of ICT within the primary curriculum:

> ...an effective ICT Co-ordinator can influence the range of ICT use by suggesting contexts within the long term planning for other subjects. It is also important for senior managers in schools to recognise staff can do much to help themselves in this respect by sharing ideas and supporting one another with resources.
>
> (OfSTED 2004a)

Similarly in the secondary sector, the need for ICT specialists is shown in discrete ICT courses, where non-specialists do not have the subject knowledge to effectively raise standards:

> Teachers' subject knowledge remains the key to the most effective practice in specialist courses but it is often a problem in discrete ICT courses at key stage 3, where there is a high proportion of non-specialists teaching the subject. There are significant problems in the recruitment of ICT specialists in some areas of the country.

Effective training for these specialists, in all phases, is another crucial aspect of training which needs to be considered.

Barriers summarised

In summarising the barriers to effective ICT in the area of training, it is helpful to look at four sources of evidence cited in this chapter so far: the outcomes of the Mirandanet NOF evaluation, the small-scale Cambridge study into ICT in ITE, OfSTED's characteristics of good ICT training in ITE and the review of staff development in ICT in Scottish primary schools and OfSTED's subject reports. The key question in summarising the barriers is 'Can any common themes and threads be drawn out?' While phases, subjects, schools and situations all present their own individual challenges, I think is it possible to use the evidence of these diverse studies and reports to summarise, identify and hopefully overcome the barriers in this crucial area of ICT in schools:

1   The distinction between training in technical skills in using ICT and developing teachers' ability to use ICT in teaching and learning must be recognised.

2   Access for teachers to appropriate ICT resources at appropriate times is crucial.

3   Outcomes of training are most usefully measured in terms of improvements in the quality of teaching and learning, not in artificial tests or tasks.

4   The teacher's personal skills, both in terms of ICT and in terms of wider skills in studying need to be considered in the planning of training.

5   Face-to-face contact with those delivering training is essential, and a significant factor in this is the availability of ICT specialists in schools.

Overcoming barriers and identifying benefits

The advice in this section is intended for trainee teachers, serving teachers, ICT specialists, school managers and policy-makers, those who work in ITE or CPD, in fact all those who have a stake in designing ICT training. The aim is not to provide a simple 'recipe' for effective ICT training, but to explain and exemplify the main issues concerned with the five barriers as described above.

1. The distinction between training in technical skills in using ICT and developing teachers' ability to use ICT in teaching and learning must be recognised.

Most teachers teach best when they feel confident, motivated and interested by the subject they're teaching. Developing this attitude towards the teaching both of discrete ICT and other subjects using ICT is dependent on teachers receiving training which helps them develop these crucial characteristics. Therefore it is important to build both practical technical skills in using ICT hardware, software and devices (how to) and develop pedagogical knowledge in planning, teaching and assessing using ICT (when to and why). Technical skills are not more important than pedagogical knowledge, and vice versa. In fact the two are mutually dependent.

One of the factors associated with the limited success of the NOF training project was that teachers' basic skills were not considered by many training providers. With technology continuing to make progress in terms of software and the range of devices on offer ever-expanding, effective training will support teachers in learning how to use new products and how to make the best of existing and established resources. This is probably best done in a face-to-face training session and considerable differentiation will be needed within the programme to meet the diverse needs of teachers who have differing skills. Peer support can also be effective in this regard, especially as small problems often occur at times when a teacher might be able to find a colleague, but does not have time to phone a helpline or wait for help.

We know from OfSTED that significant improvements in the quality of teaching and learning in ICT in both primary and secondary schools continue to be made (OfSTED 2004a; OfSTED 2004b). However one area of pedagogy which is singled out in both phases is assessment of pupils' learning. Therefore it seems appropriate that this should be the starting point of the future development of pedagogical skills in teaching and learning using ICT. The nature, timing and type of CPD which will enable teachers to develop their pedagogical understanding may differ from the nature, timing and type of technical training. Although peer support may be important, it may be that the training should be linked in closely with other CPD and delivered as part of the primary strategy, key stage 3 strategy or 14–19 project. This should ensure that ICT pedagogy is closely linked with other pedagogy where appropriate. In addition this pedagogical development should be firmly grounded in an examination of the teacher's pedagogy which is a crucial aspect of any teacher's overall professional development.

To put this distinction in context, a good example is the use of the Microsoft presentational software PowerPoint. Most readers of this book will have experienced the best and worst that this software can offer. At one end of the scale a selection of plain slides are used in a presentation where the speaker simply reads each slide before progressing to the next. This has been termed 'death by PowerPoint' by some regular attendees at conferences. At the other end of the scale, PowerPoint can be used to present images, video and animations which support the speaker's points. As the participants react to, question and develop the seminar, the speaker is able to adapt and change the route of the presentation which is hyperlinked together more like a webpage than a liner presentation. To aim for the latter rather than the former, a teacher needs a good level of technical skill with this software, and support in making and using materials which are reasonably immediate. In addition, the use of the slides, how to use them to encourage questions, the types and lengths of video used, how to assess and give feedback to contributions, how to model good use of presentational software so pupils' understanding will develop, and many more skills, will be linked to the teacher's pedagogical approach. In this case only with both technical skills and pedagogical understanding can this resource really be used effectively in the classroom.

2. Access for teachers to appropriate ICT resources at appropriate times is crucial.

The NOF funded training initiative was linked to the NGfL project which aimed to provide computers and connectivity in schools between 1998 and 2002. Unfortunately the evaluation of the NOF training showed that at times the equipment was not in place when needed in the training programme, or teachers had insufficient time to familiarise themselves with the software and equipment before the pedagogical aspects of the training began. The laptops for teachers scheme and increased school funding for computers should ensure that future training is more appropriately resourced.

To put this in context, a teacher who is planning to use a number of websites in a teaching session needs to check the content and appropriateness of the sites before the pupils access them. The teacher might prepare lessons at home or in a workroom at school, and the ability to have quick and immediate access to the Internet means the teacher can spend time researching the lesson rather than finding a computer, logging on, etc. In addition where teachers have their own laptops, they can make collections of favourite sites, as well as saving files such as presentations for use in lessons.

3. Outcomes of training are most usefully measured in terms of improvements in the quality of teaching and learning, not in artificial tests or tasks.

Assessment methods are often the defining characteristic of a particular pedagogical approach. Both the NOF training and the ICT skills tests have imposed systems of assessment which have been competency-based – in essence the curriculum was designed to enable the trainees and teachers to pass the assessment rather than with desirable learning outcomes in terms of developing knowledge and skills in teaching and learning in mind. Although the ICT skills tests remain in place, future CPD initiatives look likely to be embedded in general staff development which is linked to the strategies, and evaluation should be, at least to some extent, through the established processes of school improvement evaluation such as school action planning and through OfSTED inspections and reports. In short, the success of the initiatives will be measured in terms of their impact on classroom practice, and on teaching and learning standards.

Considering this in the context of the use of spreadsheets as tools for collating and analysing data about pupil achievement, a teacher might collect results of tests throughout the year, and use them to analyse the progress of pupils with a view to groupings. Being able to do this activity in a test situation will have no impact on pupil learning but if it is done in a real context, it will contribute to pupils being appropriately grouped. In this way the impact of training will be authentically evident in the quality of teaching and learning, as evaluated through the school's own procedures or via external agencies like OfSTED.

4. Teachers' personal skills, both in terms of ICT and in terms of wider skills in studying need to be considered in the planning of training.

Looking at the varied experiences of Joan and Catherine earlier in the chapter, one of the most important factors to consider in planning training is that each participant will bring a different set of skills and experiences to the training. For the past 20 years, since the Internet and email began to be a fundamental tool for communication in society, there have been many opportunities for people in all professions to gain 'basic' computer skills. Many teachers have taken advantage of these, and combined with CDP have produced a teaching profession which is largely computer literate. However, with the range of software and devices available ever-expanding, the range of knowledge, skills and understanding needed continues to expand accordingly, and teachers need to be given opportunities to do this at their own pace and level of interest.

For instance, a teacher might have significant skills in photography. It might be that this teacher is more willing and able to undertake training and development in the creation of images to be used in teaching and learning. These images could be made available over the school's website (or perhaps the school virtual learning environment) as a resource for all to use.

5. Face-to-face contact with those delivering training is essential, and a significant factor in this is the availability of ICT specialists in schools.

Distance learning is a complex endeavour. For years it has been done very successfully by a number of specialists, most notably the Open University. However even within these specialist providers there is recognition of the need for some face-to-face interaction between teachers and learners. The funded training evaluation showed that the distance learning model in this context did not really work, and that where training was successful it was mainly because ICT experts in the school were able to support programmes. Therefore face-to-face elements of CPD and ITE should be prioritised.

An example of this might be a teacher who wants to use a datalogger to record temperature in a science experiment. The teacher may have received some training previously, but given that such a device might only be used two or three times a year, being able to ask questions to a locally based support person would be helpful. In addition the 'hands on' nature of such devices would make a distance learning model impractical.

Useful websites

Training and Development Agency for schools (TDA): www.tda.gov.uk – for advice and support on teacher training and continuing professional development.

Hands on Support Initiative: http://www.teachernet.gov.uk/wholeschool/ ictis/ict_teaching/hos/ – for information about the HoS initiative.

Mirandanet NOF training evaluations: http://www.mirandanet.ac.uk/tta/ – information about the outcomes of the NOF-funded training.

Laptops for teachers scheme: http://lft.ngfl.gov.uk/ – information about the scheme past and future.

References

Client (2005) Client research website: http://client.cant.ac.uk/research/casestudies/nof/. Canterbury Christ Church University College.

Cunningham, M., Kerr, K., McEune, R., Smith, P., Harris, S. (2003) *Laptops for Teachers. An Evaluation of the First Year.* DfES, London.

DfES (2004c) *Hands on Support. Guidance and Support for HOS Providers. Primary.* DfES, London.

DfES (2005) Teachernet website: http://www.teachernet.gov.uk/

McCartney, J. (2002) 'Effective Models of Staff Development in ICT.' *European Journal of Teacher Education*, 27, 1, pp.61–72.

OfSTED (2002) *Handbook for the Inspection of ITT.* OfSTED, London.

OfSTED (2004a). *Ofsted Subject Reports 2002/3. Information and Communications Technology in Primary Schools.* OfSTED, London.

OfSTED (2004b) *Ofsted Subject Reports 2002/3. Information and Communications Technology in Secondary Schools.* OfSTED, London.

Preston, C. (2004) *Learning to Use ICT in Classrooms: Teachers' and Trainers' Perspectives.* Mirandanet, Oxford.

Soler, J., Craft, A., Burgess, H. (2001) *Teacher Development. Exploring Our Own Practice.* Paul Chapman, London.

Taylor, L. (2004) 'How Student Teachers Develop their Understanding of Teaching using ICT.' *Journal of Education for Teaching*, 30,1, pp. 43–56.

TES (2005) TES website: http://www.tes.co.uk/search/story/?story_id=397625.

TTA (2003a) *Qualifying to Teach. Handbook of Guidance.* Summer. TTA, London.

TTA (2005) ICT skills test website: http://www.tta.gov.uk/php/read.php?sectionid=275&articleid=1932. 2005.

CHAPTER 5

Learning content in ICT

Teaching, learning and content

The distinction between this chapter about content and the next about teaching and learning is crucial. This chapter is essentially about teaching materials. 'Resources' might be another way to describe it, while the next chapter is about how these resources are used in teaching and learning. However, the two are obviously very closely linked. As technology develops, the issue of content is becoming more and more important both in terms of what teachers can create and the increasing range of commercial products. It is appropriate to make it a special focus in a book like this.

What can good content do?

Curriculum Online is a website which draws together resources which are available to schools via the e-learning credits scheme (see Chapter 2). To assist teachers in using the resource there are two brochures (one for primary and one for secondary) produced by Curriculum Online. In their introductions, both list reasons why teachers should use ICT in the classroom:

> Because technology is an intrinsic part of our everyday lives, and children love to use it to play and learn. It's no surprise that ICT in the classroom has been linked with positive improvements in attainment and motivation (see next panel).
>
> There are many potential benefits to using ICT in teaching and learning:
>
> - ICT provides new ways for teachers to teach.
> - ICT enables teachers to be more creative in their lesson planning, to pool ideas and develop skills with others within the school as well as through collaboration with other schools.
> - ICT can make subjects more accessible to children and is adaptable to different learning styles, broadening their horizons and allowing them to achieve.

- ICT can help children think in a different way and be more creative in their problem-solving.
- ICT can bring lessons to life!

(Curriculum Online 2005a)

- Because we live in an ICT-dominated world

ICT in the classroom helps prepare pupils for a workplace already dominated by multimedia technologies.

- Because it develops teaching professionals

Using ICT can help enrich your classroom practice and give you the chance to develop new skills.

- Because it saves time and resources

According to the 2003 ICT in Schools survey, some 80 per cent of secondary teaching staff reported that 'ICT can help reduce teacher workload in terms of lesson preparation, planning and assessment'.

- Because it can extend your school's links with the community

ICT can create opportunities for families to work and learn together; encourage basic skills development; offer unique opportunities to bridge generation gaps; address the needs of deprived groups; and provide opportunities for employment.

(Curriculum Online 2005b)

To summarise, ICT is useful to:

- innovate
- be creative
- communicate
- be adaptive
- motivate
- develop skills for work and life
- optimise use of time and resources.

These seven reasons to use ICT will be used when explaining and discussing the ICT content in this chapter.

Literature review: Some examples of case studies on content

Sometimes teaching can be an insular business. Teachers are so busy working in their own schools and classrooms that they sometimes find it hard to keep up with developments in education more generally. But that is not to say that there is no innovative practice in classrooms. Quite the contrary, in classrooms all over the country, teachers are trying out new ideas. Through LEAs, BECTA, Nesta Futurelab and other similar organisations which are subject or phase specific, projects in classrooms are supported. Then via websites, reports, literature reviews and manifestos are published. As these websites become better known throughout the profession, it is hoped that communities of practice will grow and develop. It is on these sources that the following section of this chapter draws.

This is not intended to be an exhaustive survey of uses of different kinds of content and their application in each phase or subject. Rather it is intended as an overview of some of the possibilities in using different learning content.

Definition of terms: Types of content

Word, sound and image processing

In the Nesta Futurelab literature review on creativity, new technologies and learning, a number of possibilities are suggested for using digital technologies creatively:

1 Developing ideas: supporting imaginative conjecture, exploration and representation of ideas.

2 Making connections: supporting, challenging, informing and developing ideas by making connections with information, people, projects and resources.

3 Creating and making: engaging in making meanings though fashioning processes of capture, manipulation and transformation of media.

4 Collaboration: working with others in immediate and dynamic ways to collaborate on outcomes and construct shared knowledge.

5 Communication and evaluation: publishing and communicating outcomes for evaluation and critique from a range of audiences.

(Loveless 2002)

Back in the first years of using ICT in teaching and learning, BBC computers were used to enable pupils to 'type up' their work. Well into the 1990s many computers were still primarily being used this way, as a presentational tool. Gradually, clip art and the ability to import images (pictures, photos, diagrams, charts) from cameras and drawing programs have meant that work can be presented through images and text. Now movies and sounds are becoming easier to record and add to digital media. This is not to say that traditional 'word processing' is consigned to the dustbin of technological history, but rather the possibilities of presentational software are now far more interesting and diverse. The aim of this section is to examine the possibilities of this presentational software, which enables words, images (still and moving) and sounds to communicate in creative ways.

1. Developing ideas and making connections

Software which records and develops ideas is now widely available in a variety of forms. Ideas around 'mind mapping' have grown from their roots (Buzan Centres 2005) and have become well used in all phases. The software company Inspiration has produced 'Kidspiration', aimed at the primary phase, and a more complex version 'Inspiration', software which has facilities to record ideas and link them together in a 'flow diagram' style. In addition, images can be added to support text. In this way pupils can work collaboratively or independently to develop and record ideas without the need to write reams of text. The diagrams can be converted to text in one click, so there is no need to retype ideas in subsequent work.

2. Creating and making

Digital images are increasingly easy to capture. As digital cameras which take stills and video become simpler, cheaper and easier to use, teachers and learners make more and more use of them. In addition, software to be creative with still photos and video is becoming easier to use. Still images can be altered, using software like 'Photoshop' and added into word processing and presentational software which make the images convey even more creative ideas. In addition video can be edited; and text, music, sounds and stills added which go far beyond the shaky home movies of the 1980s. Moviemaking software is supplied as a standard element of software packages. Mac users have access to iMovie as a standard part of a software package, and PC users can use Windows MovieMaker or purchase software like Pinnacle studio.

3. Collaboration

Faster and constantly available broadband networks in schools have enabled pupils and teachers to exchange files with one another via email and central file stores in ways that have made the 'floppy disk' obsolete. Even where such systems do not exist, USB memory sticks and rewriteable CDs can be used to exchange files containing words, still and moving images and sounds. In this way, collaboration on digital projects is easier than ever.

A simple but effective example of this is might be collaboration in creating a PowerPoint presentation. Pupils could create individual parts at home or during independent time which then can be put together to form one presentation. The same principle might apply to a series of images or word processed documents, which can be shared, edited and amalgamated to produce work which genuinely reflects the ideas of all contributors.

4. Communication and evaluation

The final aspects of creativity which can be supported through word, sound and image processing software are communication and evaluation. Communication and evaluation are important aspects of the process of critical thinking which is at the heart of purposeful creativity. Commenting on and developing ideas is possible using a variety of tools which come as part of word processing packages. The ability to track changes made, add notes in margins and highlight text mean that for pupils reflecting on and evaluating their own work and the work of others is simple.

Reflection on these uses of word, sound and image processing software it is possible to see how such software can encourage creative teaching and learning which goes well beyond simple 'presentation' of ideas and to the heart of the creative process. The current focus on creative teaching and learning began in the late 1990s with the influential report to the Department of Culture, Media and Sport and the then Department for Education and Employment (NACCCE 1999). Creativity as an educational objective is now enshrined as part of the National Curriculum. It is to be hoped that these initiatives continue to drive the creative use of word, sound and image processing software.

Simulations and gaming

Back in the 1980s, when home and school computing began, there were two major uses of the computer. One was to word process, and the other was to play games. Where word processing quickly became established as a core ICT activity in schools, gaming and simulations have always remained in the periphery of the educational ICT use. However, in the 'non-educational' ICT sector, computer games have become big business. This branch of ICT, however, has to some extent attracted some adverse publicity, not only because of the content of games, but also because of the kinds of lifestyles they are supposed to encourage among children. In the Nesta Futurelab literature review of simulations and gaming (Kirriemuir and McFarlane 2004), Kerri Facer, Director of Learning Research, identifies these problems in her foreword at the beginning of the report:

> Computer games are today an important part of most children's leisure lives and increasingly an important part of our culture as a whole. We often, as adults, watch in amazement as children dedicate hours to acting as football coaches, designers of empires, controllers of robots, wizards and emperors. In the past, computer games have been dismissed as a distraction from more 'worthy' activities, such as homework or playing outside.
>
> (Kirriemuir and McFarlane 2004)

The question for teachers and educationalists then, is whether these kinds of technologies can have any worthy use in teaching and learning. The report goes on to explain that gaming and simulations can encourage some valuable skill development in the following areas:

- strategic thinking
- planning
- communication
- application of numbers
- negotiating skills
- group decision-making
- data-handling.

In addition, any teacher who has observed children playing with computer games will notice impressive levels of engagement, motivation and concentration. Given the possible educational benefits of harnessing gaming in the curriculum, it seems that this is an aspect of ICT which teachers should ignore at their peril.

For many years there have been some games and simulations occupying niches in the educational software market. One such product aimed at key stage 2 pupils is 'Crystal Rainforest', where pupils must solve number and word puzzles in order to progress through the game. Although this is popular in some schools, when compared to the presentation and complexity of 'adventure' games available on games consoles like Playstations, Crystal Rainforest is slow and rather unexciting. The question which may stem from this is, then, is there a role for these existing 'mainstream' games in teaching and learning in schools?

The Nesta Futurelab literature review sets the possible future of games in learning as part of its conclusions. The key issues concerning the use of games (as they exist currently) in schools are summarised as follows:

- The many roles and requirements of the teacher in terms of training, understanding of the game, keeping the students 'on track' and troubleshooting.
- Identifying games that may be successful or useful in a classroom situation.
- Cultural acceptance of games as media through which learning can take place.
- Compatibility with school hardware, licensing agreements, and arguably other software, eg allowing the player/user to easily port the financial results of a session on a business simulation game into Excel.
- There is a need for developers of games (and other software) aimed at the formal education sector to consider the various stakeholders involved, and to consider both their needs (and how these may be fulfilled by the game) and their reaction to such a device.

(Kirriemuir and McFarlane 2004)

The possible way forward in using games in schools is suggested in the report. This involves adapting existing games to augment 'educational' content and allowing users to save games and use data within other applications. The content should then be verified with educational organisations and support developed around the games for teachers and learners which makes links with the prescribed curriculum. This compromise between educational caveats and the existing games seems like a realistic way forward. It may be some time before schools are installing Playstations and the like, but the power of the computer game in mainstream culture is substantial and one which teachers and educationalists should not ignore.

However, the availability and application of games and simulations in the compulsory school sector, both at primary and secondary level, is still limited. Perhaps the reasons for this are in the age old distinction made in traditional pedagogies between 'work' and 'play', where one is the opposite of the other, and where work is a more valuable endeavour and where children are 'only' playing. Yet any early years practitioner will tell you that young children learn very effectively through play, and there seems no sound argument to suggest that children's ability to learn through play stops suddenly at the age of five when the play-based foundation stage curriculum gives way to the more formal National Curriculum. To ignore the distinction between work and play and to embrace the idea of gaming and simulation as valid educational activities is to open the possibilities of new and valuable ways of learning.

One example of a piece of simulation software is MediaStage, a package designed by Immersive Education which enables users to simulate a television studio, controlling sets, lighting, props and actors. In September 2003, working with the software developers, Nesta Futurelab ran a research project into the application of the software with a small group of year 8 pupils. In the report on this small-scale project published on the Nesta Futurelab website (Nesta Futurelab 2005), the team describe the potential of the software in both learning and motivational terms as 'of considerable importance'. In addition, they raise issues for further investigation of enhancing creativity and increasing the learning potential of modelling software.

Data-handling

Data-handling distinguishes itself as an authentic use of ICT in education, while other uses of ICT, it might be argued, are contrived because the same job could be effectively done without the use of ICT (and all the incumbent risks of this) organising, handling and sorting data is a job which ICT does well. From simple programs used in primary schools such as BlackCat software's 'Information

Workshop' to Microsoft's Excel and Access software, these tools are being used increasingly in schools.

Software that enables pupils to get immediate feedback about data is considered a general benefit of using ICT (BECTA 2003). For example, the simple activity of inputting data and creating a graph can support pupils' learning in mathematics.

In a recently published ICT handbook for primary school teachers (Price and Moore 2005), data-handling software is suggested to support teaching and learning of mathematical concepts and ideas. Activities are suggested where data-handling programs can support:

- accessing
- analysing
- presenting
- communicating
- testing
- confirming.

These activities are crucial to the development of effective pedagogy in mathematics, where pupils can devise and investigate numbers and data.

'Ready-made' Internet resources

The sheer amount of information on the Internet is daunting to teachers wanting to use it as a teaching resource. Even aside from the issues of safety dealt with in Chapter 3, it is very difficult to tell how much of the information available on the Internet is reliable, useful or appropriate for use as teaching and learning resources.

Increasingly, organisations such as BECTA are producing advice for teachers in how to use the Internet effectively in teaching, with a range of subject-specific advice sheets on using the Internet in both secondary and primary phases, and across a range of subjects on their website: http://www.becta.org.uk/corporate/publications/index.cfm.

In addition, the Curriculum Online website is a centrally organised and funded site: http://www.curriculumonline.gov.uk/Default.htm. It collects a range of ICT support, materials and training which are designed to 'enrich teaching and learning across the curriculum' (BECTA 2005b). This website provides a portal where teachers can browse multimedia teaching and learning materials, many of them web-based, to be purchased with their e-learning credits. The range and quality of available materials is testament both to the substantial amount of money which has been invested both by the government and the private sector in developing Internet and other multimedia resources. The portal also provides a directory of 'free' Internet resources which can be used by schools.

'Home-made' Internet resources

On the face of it, the idea of teachers making their own Internet resources sounds daunting. With a few notable exceptions, for example, Ambleside School (http://www.amblesideprimary.com/ambleweb/numeracy.htm) most teachers do not have the time or expertise to construct web pages, or make games and activities to be delivered via the Internet using programs like 'Flash'. However, with the increasing use of Virtual Learning Environments in schools, both in the primary and secondary sector, teachers can control, to some extent, the way their pupils use web-based resources.

'Virtual learning' is an increasingly common term, which means learning which takes place in a electronic environment. The most common example of this is learning which takes place in a VLE (Virtual Learning Environment) based on the Internet or on an intranet. Sometimes these VLEs are the only interface between teacher and learner, and sometimes the VLE is complementary to traditional face-to-face teaching and learning. This is often referred to a 'blended learning'.

Many VLEs have developed, at least initially, in the higher education sector, where experienced players in the distance learning market, such as the Open University, have transferred learning onto the web. Many other higher education establishments have also followed this pattern, offering what is known in Pittinsky's influential book (Pittinsky 2002) as 'click and click' distance learning or 'brick and click' blended learning. As VLEs have become more reliable and sophisticated, and as improvements in bandwidth to schools have made virtual learning more reliable, the schools sector has begun to investigate the possibilities of introducing VLEs into their teaching. Some schools are using commercially available solutions such as Blackboard and WebCT, others are using solutions provided via LEAs such as the netmedia VLE available via some regional broadband consortia. The full potential of VLEs is yet to be tapped, but there are already a number of interesting small-scale projects taking place in schools across the country (Broadhead 2005) and BECTA have set out a useful exemplification of what constitutes quality in e-learning resources (BECTA 2005).

A virtual learning environment might contain some of the following elements:

- announcements/noticeboards
- discussion boards
- email/message facility
- area for content

- links to other virtual resources
- assessments.

The ways in which teachers utilise these tools are dependent on how the VLE fits in with face-to-face teaching. For instance, a teacher might use a discussion board in a session, and ask the pupils to summarise the discussion as homework. Some teachers might use the VLE to deliver a web-based task such as a game or some research, as in the VLE a teacher can give pupils links to follow. In addition, most VLEs have a 'notepad' where pupils can keep notes during some research, which they might feed back to the teacher at the end of the lesson.

A major benefit of using content delivered via a VLE over using content delivered via the Internet is that pupils' progress can be easily monitored, including which content they have accessed, and when they have accessed it. Although some teachers find this 'big brother' aspect of the VLE toolkit slightly unsettling, it can be useful in monitoring pupil progress and devising appropriate intervention strategies for individuals.

Computer-based assessment is a controversial topic, which will be dealt with more fully in Chapter 6. However, many teachers are now beginning to use VLEs to set quizzes and tasks. Eventually it seems likely that more formal assessments will also take place via virtual learning environments, and at time of writing, the key stage 3 tests are being trailed in this format.

Barriers summarised

In considering what the barriers might be in this case, the first thing which occurs is the tremendous and ever-expanding range of electronic resources and equipment which are available. Even the most dedicated and ICT-savvy teacher would have trouble keeping up with developments. This leads inevitably to 'initiative overload', where teachers can no longer assimilate changes into their practice at the rate which they occur.

Another problem caused by the range of available resources is keeping classroom teachers informed of the developments in content. Although commercial companies are good at mailing (both on paper and electronically) schools, the complex systems of communications within schools means that information about new products does not necessarily get to the right teacher.

Putting aside these pragmatic concerns, there are also problems with the various types of content themselves, some of which relate to the teacher, and some to the pupils. The table below summarises the problems teachers and pupils may have with the types of content described and discussed above.

Table 5.1 Problems pupils have

Type of content	Some problems pupils have	Some problems teachers have
Word, sound and image processing	Getting bogged down in the 'mechanics' of a program, for instance spending 30 minutes of a lesson trying to get the title of a piece of work to look good. Dealing with the wide variety of file types associated with this type of software. Using a keyboard to write, the camera to record etc. Sometimes these technical issues can overwhelm a subject teaching objective.	Devising activities which utilise the full potential of software rather than simply using it as a presentational tool. Dealing with the wide variety of file types associated with this type of software. Establishing the authorship of work when pupils collaborate or are using information form other sources such as the web.
Simulations and Games	Focusing sufficiently on the learning aspects, rather than employing a 'trial and error' approach.	Identifying and promoting the desired learning objectives. Convincing other teachers/parents/pupils that gaming is an appropriate approach for learning.
Data handling	Inputting initial data – a fault with this will render all sorting, analysis and presentation work invalid.	Working beyond basic use of inputting and presenting data, and finding ways to utilise the full potential of the software in its ability to support analysis and modelling.
Ready-made Internet resources	'Web drift' – getting side-tracked from the main activity by following links on the website. Pupils with a range of special educational needs might need support in accessing some of the resources	Ready-made resources don't meet needs of pupils adequately. Knowing where to find appropriate resources.
Home-made Internet resources	Navigating and using the tools in the VLE to support learning effectively.	Learning how to use and devise appropriate resources.

The key to dealing with the majority of problems is in the teacher's pedagogical approach. Many of these problems can be overcome with what teachers might regard as ordinary 'effective teaching'.

Overcoming barriers: Developing an effective pedagogical approach

The next chapter deals in detail with effective pedagogical approaches to employ when using teaching and learning using ICT. However, considering each of these content types briefly, it is possible to devise a set of 'golden rules' for teachers in using each one.

Golden rules for using word, sound and image processing:

- Make time limits and what is to be achieved clear (including technical details such as what kind of file is to be created).
- Make expectations in terms of authorship clear. The simplest way to do this is to have a blanket policy which forbids the cutting and pasting of text and images from the Internet and CDRoms without acknowledgement. Software which detects plagiarism is also available.
- If necessary spend some time teaching the technical skills required before embarking on the subject learning objectives. However, a strong whole-school ICT skills policy should negate the need for this.

Golden rules for using simulations and games:

- Make sure pupils know the learning objectives/outcomes and are able to give feedback on these at the end of lessons.
- Focus teaching and demonstration on the problem-solving/modelling aspects of the software and tell pupils the kind of thinking you want them to engage in.

Golden rules for data-handling:

- Be clear about objectives.
- Small amounts of data, or ready inputted data can help pupils get to the stage of analysing data quicker.

Golden rules for using ready-made Internet resources:

- Have strict and monitored rules about Internet use, preferably through an acceptable use policy.
- Be clear about which websites/pages are intended to be used in the task.

- Set short, clearly defined tasks for pupils.

Golden rules for home-made Internet resources:

- Have strict and monitored rules about Internet use, preferably through an acceptable use policy.
- Be clear about which websites/pages are intended to be used in the task.
- Set short, clearly defined tasks for pupils.
- Use tools such as discussion boards, pupil monitoring systems and emails to monitor progress carefully.

Further reading: Free Internet-based content

This list is by no means exhaustive but it is hoped that it will provide a useful starting point for those who want to use Internet-based resources in teaching and learning. Teachers are increasingly able to use devices such as interactive whiteboards in their teaching, as well as sets of tablet PCs instead of traditional computer suites or a few stand-alone machines in the corner. This means that access to Internet resources is increasingly easy in classrooms, both in whole class work and in group work. The following resources may be particularly useful for use with interactive whiteboards (IWBs) or tablets, where indicated.

References

BECTA (2003) *What the Research Says About Using ICT in Maths.* BECTA, Coventry.

BECTA (2005a) *Becta's View. A Quality Framework for E-learning Resources.* BECTA, Coventry.

BECTA (2005b) *Supporting Learning and Teaching in Secondary Schools.* BECTA, Coventry.

Broadhead, E. (2005). *Blended Learning at Lady Manners School Derbyshire 14–19 Pathfinder.* DfES, London.

Buzan Centres (2005) Buzan Centres website: www.mind-map.com

Curriculum Online (2005a) Curriculum Online Brochure – Primary. BECTA, Coventry..

Curriculum Online (2005b) Curriculum Online Brochure – Secondary. BECTA, Coventry.

Kirriemuir, J. and McFarlane, A. (2004) *Literature Review in Games and Learning.* Nesta Futurelab, Bristol.

Loveless, A. (2002) *Literature Review in Creativity, New Technologies and Learning.* Nesta Futurelab, Bristol.

NACCCE (1999) *All Our Futures: Creativity, Culture and Education.* DCMS/DfEE, London.

Nesta Futurelab (2005) website: www.nestafuturelab.org.

Pittinsky, M. (2002) *The Wired Tower: Perspectives on the Impact of the Internet on Higher Education.* Financial Times/Prentice Hall, Upper Saddle River, NJ.

Price, H. and Moore, D. (2005) 'Promoting numeracy with ICT' in S. Wheeler (ed), *Transforming Primary ICT.* Learning Matters, Exeter.

Table 5.2 Freely available content

Key stage/subject	Name of resource	URL	Suggested use
Foundation Stage Communication Language and Literacy	Little animals Activity Centre	http://www.bbc.co.uk/schools/laac/menu.shtml	Ideal for independent use by children or use with a parent helper. Games, music and books designed for the Foundation Stage
Foundation Stage Knowledge and Understanding of the World	Teletubbies sliding game	http://www.bbc.co.uk/cbeebies/teletubbies/funandgames/slidinghill/	A simple game to help develop mouse or keyboard control
Key Stage 1 Mathematics	Free grids for Crick Software such as clicker	http://www.learninggrids.com/	Learning grids such as number and shape activities to go with Crick software. The site is regularly updated with new resources to inspire new lessons.
Key Stage 1 Science	The Tomato Zone	http://www.thetomatozone.co.uk/	Online resources provided by the British Tomato Growers Association. Games and activities about plants and animals.
Key Stage 2 History	The National Archive – what can we find out about Tudor life?	http://www.tudorbritain.org/	Materials, games and information to support a topic about the Tudors
Key Stage 2 English	Poem maker	http://www.mape.org.uk/activities/index.htm	Downloadable resource which can support children in constructing poems
Key Stage 3 Art	Scran – an image resource	http://www.scran.ac.uk/co/art_and_design/	Images which can be downloaded for free and support for pupils developing understanding of the work of other artists
Key Stage 3 Religious Education	The Muslim Educational Trust	http://www.muslim-ed-trust.org.uk/	Fact sheets and information available about a range of issues related to Islam
Key Stage 4 Mathematics	Discovering Egypt	http://www.discoveringegypt.com	Games and activities which take a fresh look at algebra
Key Stage 4 English	Converse website	http://aspirations.english.cam.ac.uk/converse/home.acds	A range of interactive activities to support learning about English literature
Key Stage 4 Modern foreign languages	Atantot	http://www.atantot.com/menu.htm	Activities for the Interactive Whiteboard in French and German

CHAPTER 6

Teaching and learning using technology

Background and introduction

Back in 1980, during the first exploratory years of ICT in education, an American academic, Seymour Papert, published a revolutionary book about using ICT in education. The first edition of this book *Mindstorms* has become a 'classic' in terms of learning technology (Papert 1980). In the book Papert sets out his manifesto for effective teaching and learning using ICT. Although the context of the book is largely mathematical, what Papert advocates is the use of ICT to promote authentic learning through problem-solving. The book was updated in 1993, but the first paragraph of the introduction reads, to me, as if it were written only yesterday:

> Just a few years ago, people thought of computers as expensive and exotic devices. Their commercial and industrial uses affected ordinary people, but hardly anyone expected computers to become part of day-to-day life. This view has changed dramatically and rapidly as the public has come to accept the reality of the personal computer, small and inexpensive enough to take its place in every living room or even every breast pocket. The appearance of the first rather primitive machines in this class was enough to catch the imagination of journalists and produce a rash of speculation about life in the computer rich world to come...Most writers emphasised using computers for games, entertainment, income tax, electronic mail, shopping and banking. A few talked about the computer as a teaching machine.
>
> (Papert 1993, p. 3)

Papert is acknowledged as a visionary in the field of learning technology. His vision was one in which computers not just supported learning but actually extended it. The learning environment created by his 'Logo' program was to be one where children engaged in real ways with real projects and developed a real understanding. This was not to be theoretical or wrote learning, this was to be authentic learning. He sets out his aim clearly:

I believe that certain uses of very powerful computational technology and computational ideas can provide children with new possibilities for learning, thinking, and growing emotionally as well as cogitatively.

(Papert 1993, p. 4)

Although this book sets out to be positive about ICT in education, it would be wrong to suggest that it has been demonstrated that ICT has had a transformative effect on education thusfar. *The big pICTure* (DfES 2003b), the DfES published report, which collates most recent and influential research into teaching and learning, has difficulty in making a real case for a positive relationship between ICT and improved teaching and learning. Some of the reasons for this are related to the methodologies of educational research, in that it has been difficult to separate the effects of good teaching, school management and ICT, as the three often occur together. Another problem which *The big pICTure* has in making a convincing case is the nature of the data used. Many of the studies rely heavily on formal testing of children's knowledge and skills in SATs or public exams, and as any teacher will tell you, the relationship between actual test scores and real ability is often tenuous. Where the conclusions rely on case studies and qualitative data, the studies are often small scale and the findings cannot be reliably extrapolated into a wider context.

In short, we are yet to gather the evidence which proves the authentic learning – which Papert calls for in *Mindstorms* – is really happening in our schools. This raises three important questions:

1   What *is* ICT being used for in schools?
2   What might it be used for?
3   Is Papert's vision a realistic or desirable one?

This chapter examines, in detail, these three questions and sets out how teachers, schools and educationalists can move towards using ICT in valuable and authentic ways in teaching and learning.

Definition of terms

In order to examine and discuss teaching and learning using ICT it is first necessary to be clear about definitions. One of the biggest barriers to effective ICT is the bewildering range of terms used to describe the activities which take place. This section aims to explain some of these terms, under six headings:

1   Basic skills
2   Skills with text
3   Skills with images

4   Skills with data-handling

5   Gaming and problem-solving skills

6   Creative and thinking skills.

For the purposes of this chapter, I intend to deal with these skills thematically, but in the National Curriculum level descriptors, the skills are set out incrementally, in the order in which children are likely to be able to master them. The level descriptors are useful for teachers both to assess pupils' learning and to plan for progression.

Basic skills

Basic skills are the generic ones needed to use a computer or other ICT device: mouse control, keyboard skills, printing, creating files and organising work, connecting and using peripherals such as cameras and scanners. In addition, pupils should be able to choose the appropriate use of ICT for a task, in terms of choosing the right application and tools for the job.

Skills with text

Skills with text might include changing the size, type and design of text and organising and formatting text on a page. Related skills are creating and using tables, bullet points and numbering to organise text.

Skills with images

Adding images to documents is relatively easy, but there are a number of ways in which images need to be prepared before adding them to documents. Choosing the right file type is crucial to keeping file sizes reasonable, in addition images need to be resized before adding them to documents.

There is now a variety of ways to create digital images. As well as using a camera to take still and moving pictures, images can be scanned from 'hard copies'. Creating images using software is also increasingly effective with drawing tools becoming more sophisticated.

Skills with data-handling

Data, once inputted, can be sorted, organised and presented in various ways. In addition, using dataloggers in scientific and mathematical activities means that there are some skills in collecting data in this way. Reliability of information and being able to spot and interpret problems with data is also important in effectively using ICT in data handling.

Gaming and problem-solving skills

These skills are used in a variety of contexts. Being able to control a game using keys or a joystick requires good hand–eye co-ordination. Making choices using

ICT is a skill pupils need to learn early on. In addition, there are a number of skills in understanding and solving problems which occur in games. A good memory and a good knowledge of the workings of computer games are important skills. Most gamers also come with a range of built-in 'cheats' which can be learned and used.

Creative and thinking skills

The ease with which moving images and music can be made and used has opened new possibilities in working creatively using computers. Video can be easily edited and music and effects added to allow the creation of imaginative productions. An important skill in being creative is knowing which tools to use in which situations, depending on the desired effects. Audio files can be published easily through podcasting. This term derives from the near-ubiquitous Macintosh ipod music player, and describes an audio file which is downloaded from the Internet and then can be played on an MP3 (audio file) player. This easy way of publishing both original music and voice creations can be a great incentive for pupils in producing work in this way.

Case studies in teaching and learning

As the introduction briefly examined, finding a single piece of evidence which demonstrates that teaching and learning with ICT is effective is impossible. Despite a substantial and rapidly growing body of research into educational technology, it is difficult to isolate ICT as an important factor in good standards of teaching and learning. Often good use of ICT goes hand in hand with good teaching methods, and this is often against a background of effective school management in general. Ethics in educational research preclude the 'control group' approach. It would be thought by the majority of educational researchers highly unethical to, for instance, take a cohort of children, give one half access to high-quality ICT and deprive the other half. For this reason, the majority of educational research falls into two categories. The type based on qualitative data such as test scores and exam results, and the type based on usually small-scale case studies. Both of these approaches have intrinsic drawbacks, but this is the evidence we have. Eventually it is hoped that enough momentum will be built up and enough evidence will be gathered for us to say that ICT is effective in promoting high-quality teaching and learning.

Issues and case studies in assessment

Assessment is in itself often a controversial issue in schools. Some teachers and educationalists regard our current educational system as driven by the modes of assessment we use. Our pupils in England and Wales are perhaps among the most assessed in the world. The links between assessment standards and the accountability of the education system have become so established it seems unlikely that any future Secretary of State for Education would take radical action to substantially reduce the load. This has resulted in controversy building up around the issue of assessments in the public domain, some of which has gone beyond sensible consideration into the realms of hysteria, where there are annual calls for the return of the 'good old days' of exams on every front page, special news report and webpage:

> There is a far bigger blight on interesting and exciting developments in education than there is in medicine, or architecture even. Powerful retro rockets propelling us back to the past make teachers feel guilty if they innovate, or challenge the status quo.
>
> Fear of the annual August results circus can drive imagination into a deep trench. Older generations would remember what is involved in creative teaching and the more robust would have a go. The rest would believe schools were failing. Only the past can save us.

(Wragg 2005)

However, progress and development of the assessment and exams system does not have to lead us back to the past. A good example is the assessment for learning initiative (DfES 2005e) and the major overhaul of the public exams system which is proposed in the 14–19 agenda (DfES 2004f) which has begun to set out a case for rethinking the nature of assessment in schools.

Essentially there are two modes of assessment, formative and summative. Although not all assessment procedures fit neatly into one or other of these categories, these definitions are helpful in examining the nature of assessment.

Characteristics of formative assessment:

- provides feedback to teachers and pupils about skills and knowledge;
- can be useful in diagnosing gaps in knowledge or skills;
- is sometimes undertaken repeatedly to track progress;
- allows pupils to have some input into the nature and timing of assessments.

Characteristics of summative assessments:

- results are sometimes not fully shared with pupils;
- used to provide a 'snapshot' of attainment at a particular time;
- is undertaken at the end of a unit of learning;
- nature and content is defined by teachers and often kept secret from pupils until they take the assessment.

Computers and assessment

Using computers for assessment has been possible for some time. Back in the days of programming in 'Basic' on Sinclair home computers it was possible to set simple quizzes using the 'if' command. Computer-aided tests and exams have since become commonplace, especially in further and higher education (Pittinsky 2002) and in the United States in particular.

However, this model of computer-aided assessment is only part of what is possible using computers now, and a number of initiatives are underway which will mean that modes of assessment will be more strongly linked with ICT applications in the future. Nesta Futurelab's literature review on e-assessment sets out the forms which e-assessment might take:

> E-assessment can take a number of forms, including automating administrative procedures; digitising paper-based systems, and online testing – which extends from banal multiple choice tests to interactive assessments of problem-solving skills.
>
> (Ridgeway and McCusker 2004)

The review firmly states that the question is not if e-assessment will play a role but 'what, when and how'. Therefore, as teachers and educationalists, we must examine how e-assessment might contribute to good quality teaching and learning in our schools. As with all applications of ICT, it is important to consider the advantages and disadvantages of e-assessment over existing paper-based procedures:

Advantages of e-assessment:

- In an educational system which increasingly involves ICT in teaching and learning, having computer-aided assessment seems an appropriate pedagogical choice.
- E-assessment can be tailored to meet the needs of individual pupils in terms of the type and timing of assessments.
- E-assessment can give immediate and detailed feedback to pupils.
- Although the jury is still very much out on the positive effects of ICT on teaching and learning, one area in which links have been firmly established is in the positive effects of ICT on pupil motivation (DfES 2003b) – therefore it may be that pupils are well-motivated to take e-assessments.
- Because e-assessments can generate data about results quicker than traditional paper-based methods, data can be used more immediately to plan the next stages of teaching and learning for individuals, whether this is in the context of pupils moving into further and higher education or planning lessons for the next week.

Disadvantages of e-assessments:

- Teachers and learners might need to learn new skills to create, access and use the formats.
- Some electronic assessment systems rely too heavily on systems of assessment like 'multiple choice' and 'fill in the blank'.
- Electronic assessments can be unreliable if the technology supporting them is not sufficiently robust.
- Some electronic formats could exclude some users with visual impairments or other disabilities.

In weighing up these advantages and disadvantages, teachers considering using e-assessment need to consider the specific situation and assessment they want to make. In learning environments which use both face-to-face teaching and virtual learning there is a place for both traditional and e-assessment. Best practice might be that some assessments are made in one way and some in the other, and therefore, it is hoped, making the best of both situations. Some possible examples of formative and summative e-assessment are set out below:

Examples of formative e-assessment

The wealth of online content now available to teachers (see Chapter 5) has also included some online tests and tasks which pupils can use in lessons. A good range of these are available on the BBC website. The 'revisewise' site is designed to enable pupils to revise knowledge for SATs and exams. An example of a simple online test for key stage 2 science is available at: http://www.bbc.co.uk/apps/ifl/schools/gigaquiz?path=ks2revisewise/14_test&infile=14_test.

Although this multiple-choice format has its disadvantages, when multichoice testing is part of a wider pedagogical approach it can be helpful to enable pupils to test their knowledge. In addition there are a number of games on the site, which while designed as 'light relief' from revision, can consolidate pupils' ability to use their knowledge in different contexts.

However, tests and tasks are not the only way ICT can be used for formative assessments. Electronic portfolios are being flagged by the producers of Virtual Learning Environments (VLEs) as the 'next big thing' in e-assessment. Essentially, an e-portfolio is a collection of digital media which can be used by learners to demonstrate their skills and knowledge. The advantage of this over a paper-based portfolio is that a wide range of media, including text, still and moving images, spreadsheets and graphs, can be used to demonstrate knowledge and understanding. In addition, because e-portfolios can be created in the VLE and both teachers and pupils can view the work under construction and before final presentation, a dialogue can be established about the portfolio, which does not rely on teachers taking home piles of paper, or on waiting for feedback until the next taught session. Electronic portfolios have begun to be used in further and higher education in the USA. There are a range of projects, which are detailed online at: http://ctl.du.edu/portfolioclearinghouse/search_portfolios.cfm.

Examples of summative e-assessment

As previously discussed, summative assessment is an element of the dominant pedagogy of schools which seems to be here to stay. However, there are some current initiatives to rethink aspects of the summative assessment system utilising some of the advantages which e-assessment can offer.

An interesting example of summative electronic testing is the 'World Class Tests project', which is designed to identify 'gifted and talented'. Whether or not such tests can identify pupil talent effectively might be open to question, but the nature and format of the tests is an interesting departure from a simple multiple choice format. The following test, aimed at older primary pupils who may be talented in mathematics is a good example: http://www.worldclassarena.org/v5/example_questions.htm#.

The first formal use of e-assessment will be the key stage 3 ICT tests, which are, at the time of writing, being trialled in some schools. This project is, it seems, to be the forerunner of further projects to develop e-assessment in schools. Details of the new key stage 3 ICT test can be found at: http://www.qca.org.uk/7280.html

A less successful use of e-assessment is the Qualified Teacher Status (QTS) Tests in English, Mathematics and ICT which all those seeking to acquire QTS must pass. There is a perception among the teacher training community that these tests are, to some extent, contrived and very controversial (Anon 2004) but there are, at the time of writing, no plans to abolish the tests: http://www.tda.gov.uk/skillstests/practicematerials.aspx.

Teachers can already use free software to create online tests. One example is 'Hot Potatoes' which is a free quiz generator, available to download from the Internet. Quizzes may then be delivered as part of a VLE or hosted on a website: http://www.hotpotatoes.info/questions.htm.

In conclusion, these case studies show that there is a wide variety of applications for e-assessment and that when it is used appropriately, it can make a significant impact on teaching and learning. These examples might not be useful or applicable in all situations, but their diversity does indicate that there is a wide range of projects developing e-assessment methods. It is to be hoped that projects such as those above form a basis for electronic assessment practice in the future, where assessment becomes an integrated aspect of, but not the driver of, pedagogical innovation.

Issues and case studies in individualised learning

Every day, in every classroom, in every country, every teacher is faced with the same situation: a class, a group, a collection of individuals whom they must teach. And in this dichotomy lies probably the biggest problem every teacher faces: how to teach the *whole group* in a way which helps each *individual* to make good progress. This is such a big problem for teachers, pupils and everyone else in education, that if there were an easy answer to this issue, someone would surely have discovered it by now.

Despite the magnitude of the problem, the issue of personalised learning has only recently begun to be important in the educational agenda. The standards website, run by the DfES, has some considerable space devoted to the issue (DfES 2005e) and has begun what they are describing as 'a conversation' about 'personalised' learning (DfES 2004g). This is being driven, to some extent, by the 14–19 curriculum reform agenda (DfES 2004f). It is also related to the issues raised by the inclusion agenda, which aims to include in 'mainstream' education pupils who might, in the past, have been excluded from mainstream education because of their special needs, medical needs, geographical location or problems with behaviour. In addition, there is some work being done at the moment into how ICT can reduce teacher workload, which should at least in theory, enable teachers to spend more time devising individual programmes of work for pupils (DfES 2003a).

There have been a number of small-scale studies on individualised learning programmes and ICT hardware and software which can support teachers in meeting pupils' individual needs in a range of contexts.

VLEs in supporting absent pupils and staff

Virtual Learning Environments (VLEs) are becoming more and more popular in schools. While some schools are using commercially produced solutions, many schools are opting for 'open source' VLEs such as Moodle http://moodle.org/.

One such school in the north-east, Egglescliffe, uses the VLE in a range of teaching and learning contexts. The VLE has been used by teachers during periods of absence to maintain contact with pupils (Krechowiecka 2005). There are also some VLEs supporting pupils who are absent from school. Research in this area has been pioneered by the 'Not School' project, which aims to re-engage young people back into education, who have, for whatever reason, been excluded or absent from school: http://www.notschool.net.

Essentially, communicating school work over distance can be done without a VLE. For many years absent teachers and pupils have communicated by post, phone and even, in remote locations like the Scottish islands, by radio. Teachers and pupils working together outside the school building is far from a new concept. However, such VLE projects can add a valuable new dimension. Using a

VLE has many advantages over previous systems which teachers and pupils have used to communicate outside school:

- VLEs utilise technology such as computers, digital imaging and podcasting. Research suggests that pupils find using ICT motivating (DfES 2003b), so pupils who might be absent because of disaffection may be more likely to engage in learning.

- VLEs allow teachers and pupils to communicate by email and messaging systems such as discussion boards. Because these systems can be used in synchronous and asynchronous ways, timescales for communication can be flexible, meeting the needs of teachers and pupils.

- VLEs enable teachers to track pupils' use of the system, so they can see which elements of the VLE have been used by pupils, for how long and when. This enables teachers to monitor pupils' learning much more closely, as they would in a traditional classroom. This is helpful in teachers developing and understanding of pupils' learning styles and approaches.

- VLEs can enable pupils to produce work in a variety of formats, including video, text and audio files. This multimedia approach enables pupils to produce more creative work.

ICT and social inclusion

'Social inclusion' has become an important political issue over the past few years. It is a recurrent theme in social and educational policy. Loosely defined, social inclusion policies attempt to overcome social and educational barriers which prevent people achieving their potential. There have been some recent studies into how ICT can assist in this process (BECTA 2005c), which look at projects in schools where ICT has contributed to overcoming barriers and assisting social inclusion in a variety of ways:

- ICT has been useful in motivating pupils in their learning, and has given pupils the opportunity to practice and rehearse skills.

- The ability of ICT to deliver learning materials which are multisensory helps pupils with a variety of learning styles.

- ICT has supported pupils who are developing English as an additional language by providing opportunities to learn in English and in their home language across the curriculum.

- ICT can allow children to experience learning in a variety of ways, including play and other engaging activities.

- ICT can support schools in developing good links with parents and carers to encourage participation in children's learning at home.

The BECTA report puts a positive spin on this issue, demonstrating that ICT can have a positive effect on social inclusion. Ten years ago ICT could have been seen as something which was socially exclusive, given the expense involved in buying a PC and connecting to the Internet. But as various technologies have become more affordable and training and support for all in using ICT has become more readily available through adult education and through organisations like the BBC, ICT has become accessible to all.

It is a standing joke in many homes across the UK that when adults have problems with working the computer, programming the DVD player to record a TV programme or sending a text message, they look to the younger members of the household for help. Any adult who has watched an eight year old confidently send a text message, or a teenager learn a complex computer game in two hours must be struck by how children have assimilated ICT devices into their lives. The most recent and comprehensive study surveyed over 1800 children aged between five and 18 about how computers affected their lives (Hayward, Alty, *et al.* 2003). The report outlines pupils' experiences of computers and how having access to a computer at home and school affected their learning. Although the overall picture is inconclusive, the statistic data points to both parents and children considering ICT to have a positive effect on learning.

In the future, school ICT provision is likely to expand into mobile devices such as handheld computers and tablet PCs, which, easily transportable between home and school, will no doubt have a significant impact on the way pupils learn. Such devices, which will be available to all pupils, should further the kinds of social inclusion as described above.

ICT devices for pupils with special educational needs

There is an increasing number of studies which analyse the impact of ICT on teaching and learning, which continue to try to secure a link between ICT and improvements in teaching and learning (Harrison, Comber, *et al.* 2002; DfES 2003b; BECTA 2003c). The balance of evidence points to ICT having (at least) no negative impact on overall standards achieved by pupils, and some positive effect on attainment. However, most of these general studies do not look in detail at the impact of ICT on pupils with special educational needs. Given the strong influence of the inclusion agenda on schools, this looks like a serious omission.

One visit to the Special Needs ICT Exhibition, held yearly in association with the *Times Educational Supplement*, demonstrates the huge range of ICT devices available to support the learning of pupils with special needs (Galloway 2004). The range of both hardware and software aimed specifically at pupils with special needs, some developed by specialist companies and some by leading ICT companies, is impressive:

Hardware

- Specialised keyboards for those with physical impairments.
- A wide variety of mice, including rollerballs and devices such as pointers
  and switch................... l to pupils who find it the
  .... e difficult.
- .... eful for those with learning,
- .... mmunication impairments.

So.................................
- .... acquisition of basic skills
- .... rough symbols to support
- .... upport pupils with dyslexia.

.... e of needs in mainstream and
spe................ upils with special needs find
using ICT as motivational as other pupils, and the power of ICT to support pupils in overcoming communication difficulties should enable pupils to play a full role in the learning and social life of schools.

Issues of individualised and personalised learning are likely to be an important issue for all schools in the future. Three issues are discussed above, including absent pupils and teachers, social inclusion and ICT to support pupils with special educational needs. These three issues are also closely linked with whole school development and are likely to be on every school's development plan agenda. In this way the importance of successful ICT is exemplified – it can help schools have success in many important areas, and help teachers cope with the age-old problems of balancing the needs of individuals while teaching groups.

Issues and case studies in creative uses of technology

Creativity is, at the time of writing, an educational 'buzz word'. Since the first report in the area (NACCCE 1999) creativity has been something which many schools and teachers have sought to include in their teaching. Even the National Curriculum has been re-branded as creative: http://www.ncaction.org.uk/creativity/index.htm.

However, in examining the possible links between ICT and creativity, it is necessary to first examine what might be considered to be 'creative' teaching and learning. The National Curriculum in Action website defines the characteristics of creativity in teaching and learning in four main areas:

First, they (the characteristics of creativity) always involve thinking or behaving *imaginatively*. Second, overall this imaginative activity is *purposeful*: that is, it is directed to achieving an objective. Third, these processes must generate something *original*. Fourth, *the outcome must be of value* in relation to the objective.

(DfES 2005g)

Some may argue with this definition, but it is useful in considering how ICT can promote creativity. The growth of the creativity agenda has, at least, given teachers and educationalists the opportunity to develop their practice and bring to the curriculum some of the opportunities which have, until relatively recently, been precluded by the prescriptive nature of the National Curriculum. In short, it has given opportunities to develop both the content and the methods of teaching and learning in ways which have helped teachers make the curriculum more enjoyable and meaningful for themselves and their pupils. The links between these teaching and learning opportunities and digital technologies are discussed in the Nesta Futurelab report on creativity, new technologies and learning:

> What is the role of digital technologies in these processes? Digital information and communications technologies (ICT) can be seen as a set of tools which can be chosen as and when they are appropriate in the creative process. In addition, it can be argued that the characteristics of ICT can also make a distinctive contribution to those processes, providing new tools, media and environments for learning to be creative and learning through being creative. Learners and teachers can use ICT to support imaginative expression, autonomy and collaboration, fashioning and making, pursuing purpose, being original and judging value. ICT can offer opportunities to be creative in authentic contexts in ways which have not been as accessible or immediate without new technologies. Such accessibility and flexibility, however, present challenges to teachers and schools in confronting present models of resources, timetables, curriculum and assessment requirements, which can inhibit learners' engagement with creative processes and lead to a superficial or fragmented focus on products.
>
> (Loveless 2002)

This illustrates a central dichotomy of teaching using ICT, which is also the central dichotomy of this book: the tension between the benefits of using ICT and the barriers to using it. Loveless characterises these barriers as 'challenges', and all those who have seen ICT used in teaching and learning may well recognise these, technical, pedagogical and curriculum challenges. However, Loveless makes the case in the report that the very nature of some new digital technologies can allow for some modes of teaching and learning which are very well suited to encouraging creativity. It is well worth the effort needed to overcome the barriers and the challenges in this case.

Possible activities to encourage creativity through the use of ICT

The following is a set of general activities which can be adapted across the range of key stages and subjects. They are arranged under four headings, using the definition of creativity from the National Curriculum in Action website, as above.

Activities to encourage imaginative work

Many people think that 'play' is the opposite of 'work'. Teachers, especially those who have trained to teach in the foundation stage and early primary years know different – that play is the work of young children. In essence what ICT can allow pupils to do is to play with ideas: to create, to alter, amend and experiment. In a context where words, images, music and movies can easily be subjected to changes, pupils are more likely to allow their imaginations to develop new ideas. A good example of this is in moviemaking. Digital video is easily recorded and transferred into editing software, which is simple enough to be used even by primary school children. Asking children to make a video to communicate an idea, for instance a science concept or poem, will spark a creative approach when pupils can easily change the way the movie appears, and alter colours, speeds and effects. Video can be cut and reorganised and music, sound effects and commentary can be easily added. Because many effects and changes can be done and undone at the touch of a button or a click of a mouse, ICT can support imaginative experiment.

Activities to encourage purposeful work

The effects of ICT on motivation of pupils have been widely researched (DfES 2003b). There exists reasonably conclusive evidence that ICT can have a number of effects on the ways pupils relate to their work in terms of engagement, attention levels and feeling they have a purpose for their work (Passey, Rogers, *et al.* 2003). This may be because ICT enables pupils to work in contexts which are more 'real'. One example of this is a project in the East of England where pupils have been able to create and develop their own news network. Pupils have developed journalistic and collaborative skills in this project run by the East of England Broadband Consortium: http://kmi4schools.e2bn.net/mtn_central/.

ICT also facilitates communication and collaboration over work which many pupils find motivating. Getting feedback from and engaging in discussion with peers and teachers can give pupils immediate feedback on their ideas and help them feel valued.

Activities to encourage original work

In the past, some aspects of the educational system have valued uniformity over originality. Pupils in the same classes have done the same work and produced very similar outcomes. In some situations, this is an appropriate pedagogical approach. Where skills and knowledge of pupils are compared with one another in tests and examinations, it has seemed fair to have the same or similar expectations of all pupils. However, there is increasing scope for pupils to demonstrate their ideas, knowledge and skills in a variety of contexts. The increasing use of coursework as a mode of assessment has, to some extent at least, given pupils opportunities to produce more original responses than they would in a traditional examination. ICT supports pupils in creating original work because it allows imaginative and creative presentation of work, but ICT can also allow pupils to genuinely produce original responses to questions. An example of this can be the creation of data handling files and spreadsheets to manage data. Pupils can set up their own ways of dealing with complex data using these tools, and come to original conclusions about the data easily, by simply using the software to manipulate the data. In short ICT can do the 'lower order' skills such as simple calculation of results, and allow pupils to move quickly to 'higher' order skills such as interpreting data. In this way, pupils are more likely to be able to come to original conclusions than if they had been bogged down in mechanistic tasks.

Activities to encourage work of value

All teachers know that valuing what pupils produce is vital in an effective teaching and learning relationship. Where pupils feel their contributions are well-received, they are more likely to contribute. For many years in traditional pedagogies, the only person to see a pupil's work would have been their teacher, or if they were lucky, other pupils might see the work if selected for display in the classroom. ICT has changed this situation entirely. The power of networked computers and the Internet has enabled pupils to publish their work to their peers and to the wider educational community. This might mean written work, images, movies or music they have created. Possibilities continue to expand, as podcasting (see above) and blogging (weblogs, which can be updated easily and commented upon by readers) become more easily accessible. These new uses of ICT mean that in the future the audience for pupils' work will be much wider than their teachers or their class. Good work will be valued by friends, family and the whole educational community to which that pupil belongs. Blogging, an easy way to publish text and images on the Internet, is becoming increasingly popular for groups to share ideas or for individuals to publish thoughts and ideas. Both Typepad and Blogger provide web space for this purpose free of charge.

As the issues connected with creative teaching and learning are further examined in research, it seems likely that the contribution of ICT to the creativity agenda will be significant.

Issues raised and barriers summarised

Considering the three pedagogical themes discussed above – assessment, individualised learning and creativity – there are a number of key themes and barriers which emerge in terms of teaching, learning, curriculum and pedagogical approach.

- The curriculum is a constraint. The National Curriculum is nearly 20 years old at the time of writing, and despite some significant reviews and developments of strategies and schemes of work to support it, it is still based largely on a traditional academic model. If the theories of individualised learning are to be fully developed, a curriculum which allows for more freedom is needed. This is also true of the creativity agenda.

- Modes of assessment are intrinsically linked to the curriculum, one feeding the other. In some significant portions of children's school experience, what they learn and the way in which they learn it is driven by the need for them (and their schools) to succeed in examinations. While the examination system depends on summative and prescribed tests, the curriculum will be constrained by them.

- The need for pupils to succeed in the current examinations system dictates that they must practice undertaking forms of assessment which mirror the approach of these all-important exams. This leads to inertia in assessment, the curriculum and pedagogical approaches.

- Schools' spaces and resources are not ideally organised to allow maximum use to be made of ICT. Computer suites have little space for other resources and access to them can be limited. A school timetable which splits the day into arbitrary sections of time can restrict creative approaches to teaching and learning. Although significant amounts of money have been invested in ICT in schools over the past ten years, many schools still find it difficult to invest in the technologies they need to support them, and many teachers and managers lack appropriate training that would enable them to make the best of the technology they already have in their schools.

Overcoming the barriers and unlocking the benefits in teaching and learning with ICT

Given the barriers identified above, it is clear that fundamental changes to teaching, learning, the curriculum, the school day and resources are needed. However, there are things which teachers can do which can, in small ways, help them overcome some of the barriers. These might be things which teachers can do in the short term or things which need more planning. The following table is a selection of examples:

Table 6.1 Examples of simple changes to teaching and learning strategies

Foundation Stage	Integrating ICT and play	Increasingly sturdy ICT appliances such as CD players, cameras and robots are available for children to use in their play.
		Foundation Stage practitioners should plan to integrate such devices into play and practical activities wherever possible, for example, using a camera to record outdoor games, so children can teach each other games, or adding remote control toys such as cars to the small world play area.
Key Stage 1	Teaching and learning basic ICT skills	Key to pupils being able to use ICT effectively is their mastery of basic ICT skills, such as using a camera, operating a mouse, using a keyboard and understanding how to print, save and open documents in common programs. For this reason KS1 teachers should have a program where children can learn such skills. The best way to do this is to practice them a little but often. Ten minutes' practice once a week in using a keyboard is significantly more effective than an hour once a half-term. KS1 teachers might find the teaching of these simple skills a useful way to use extra classroom help such as parent helpers.
		Children are motivated by achievements in this area and teachers might set up a range of rewards or certificates for pupils who have mastered basic skills.
Key Stage 2	Encouraging independent learning through ICT	As pupils progress through KS2, they become more able to work independently of the teacher. ICT can support this by enabling pupils to work in media in which they can demonstrate this independence – a pupil might not be ready to communicate information about a project, for instance a geography study on the local area, in written prose, but a number of digital photographs supported by captions and perhaps put into an electronic presentation will communicate their findings equally effectively.
		In addition, the opportunity to use ICT motivates many pupils to push their learning forward and work collaboratively.
Key Stage 3	ICT as a tool for communication in developing a wider view of the world.	As pupils begin their secondary school level education, they are often moving from a small educational community to a larger one. For some pupils this can be daunting, and developing a sense of their own value and position within that community is crucial.

110

Table 6.1 Examples of simple changes to teaching and learning strategies (continued)

		ICT can help pupils communicate, through chat rooms, discussion and email within their community. Older pupils might be able to help younger pupils with work, and electronic communication would ease some of the practical problems of getting such pupils together.
		Electronic communication can give valuable opportunities to communicate outside the school as well. As pupils' horizons broaden, ICT can be used to communicate with teachers and learners from the wider educational community, perhaps in the local area but also further afield nationally and internationally. Where teachers can give purpose to this, whether to support language development or to research other pupils' lives, this sort of communication can be very valuable.
Key Stage 4	Using ICT as an effective tool in assessment	In KS4, pupils and teachers become closely focused on exams and coursework. ICT can support teaching and learning during this period.
		Formative testing and quizzes can be helpful to teachers in assessing pupils' knowledge, and computer-generated quizzes can generate statistical data about individuals and groups and their knowledge and understanding, which teachers can use in planning teaching sessions.
		In addition, pupils can use formative testing to assess their own knowledge and understanding. Although such formats have their drawbacks, many pupils find these helpful.
Key Stage 5	ICT and study skills	In moving into further and higher education, pupils might encounter the need to develop a new set of study skills.
		ICT is able to support pupils in learning how to research independently, as many sources of information are now available electronically on the Internet, from scientific reports to reviews of plays and books.
		ICT can also support pupils in organising and presenting their findings, and there are some useful programs available to store quotes, notes and to allow information to be easily used in pupils own essay and report writing.
		If pupils begin to develop these study skills in KS5, they will find the transition from school to FE and HE smoother, as well as the independent study benefiting their studies and exams.

Further reading

There is a range of ICT books giving practical advice to teachers and trainees on using ICT, along with a number of websites which can support teaching and learning. This is not intended to be an exhaustive list, but a starting point for readers to further pursue the ideas raised in this chapter.

Books which raise important issues

Books about ICT can date fast. ICT moves at such a pace that authors can have trouble keeping up with changes which happen during the period of writing, never mind developments which happen post-publication. This is not to say that older books about ICT are irrelevant as some have stood the test of time. The following two books are examples of a recently produced book which covers a wide range of ICT issues, and a much older yet still highly relevant text. Although there have been many books about teaching and learning with ICT published in between these two, these are simple examples of their genres:

Transforming Primary ICT, edited by Steve Wheeler (Wheeler 2005), raises many important issues relating to teaching ICT in primary schools. It covers visual literacy, creativity, and schools of the future. Although these are in a primary school context, many are also relevant to the secondary phase.

Seymour Papert's book *Mindstorms* (Papert 1980; Papert 1993) has already been discussed in this chapter, but it warrants another mention here because it is such an important text. The fundamental ideas contained within the book remain relevant 25 years later.

Textbooks

There is also a range of textbooks about ICT which are directed mainly at the Initial Teacher Training market. These are essentially 'how to' books, which give direct and practical help in using ICT in teaching and learning.

One example of this genre is books designed to help trainees through their ICT skills test (Ferrigan 2005). This book guides trainee teachers through the process of the skills tests, giving tips and example questions. There are also similar textbooks available which are phase and subject specific.

Websites

The National Curriculum in Action website links with the curriculum and provides examples of children's work, with a commentary describing the context. Although not always reflecting the most innovative of practices, the site provides a good starting point for teachers looking for examples of what children can achieve using ICT: http://www.ncaction.org.uk/.

The Teacher Resource Exchange is a database of online resources which is moderated as part of the National Grid for Learning. It can be searched according to subjects, key stage and the purpose of the activity. The resources come with notes about how they might be used. These can be used as they are when teachers are looking for a 'quick fix', or used as the basis to develop ideas for lessons. http://tre.ngfl.gov.uk/

Where teachers are looking for innovation, and thought-provoking ideas, the Nesta Futurelab produces a series of interesting and forward-thinking reports and literature reviews on a variety of ICT-related issues such as the 14–19 agenda, creativity and assessment. These can be used when teachers and managers are planning for future ICT developments and could be useful in professional development for teachers, because of their forward thinking and optimistic tone. These reports, written by experts in the field, are also a good starting point for future research. http://www.nestafuturelab.org/

References

Anon (2004) 'Who's failing whom?' in the *Times Educational Supplement*.

BECTA (2003c) *Primary Schools – ICT and Standards*. BECTA, Coventry.

BECTA (2005c) *A Good Start. Using ICT to Enable Social Inclusion in Primary Schools*. BECTA, Coventry.

DfES (2003a) *Fulfilling the Potential: Transforming Teaching and Learning Through ICT in Schools*. DfES, London.

DfES (2003b) *The big pICTure: The Impact of ICT on Attainment, Motivation and Learning*. DfES, London.

DfES (2004f) *14–19 Curriculum and Qualifications Reform*. DfES, London.

DfES (2004g) *A National Conversation about Personalised Learning*. DfES, London.

DfES (2005e) The Standards Site.: http://www.standards.dfes.gov.uk/personalisedlearning/about/.

DfES (2005g) National Curriculum in Action Creativity website: http://www.ncaction.org.uk/creativity/index.htm.

Ferrigan, C. (2005) *The ICT Skills Test*. Exeter, Learning Matters.

Galloway, J. (2004) 'Stands Out' in the *Times Educational Supplement*.

Harrison, C., Comber, C., Fisher, T., Haw, K., Lewin, C., Luzner, E., McFarlane, A., Mavers, D., Scrimshaw, P., Somekh, B., Watling, R. (2002) *ImpaCT2: The Impact of Information and Communication on Pupil Learning and Attainment. Strand 1 Report*. DfES, London.

Hayward, B., Alty, C., Pearson, S., Martin, C. (2003) *Young People and ICT 2002*. BECTA, Coventry.

Krechowiecka, I. (2005) 'Please sir, can we have some more?' in *The Guardian*, p. 5.

Loveless, A. (2002) *Literature Review in Creativity, New Technologies and Learning*. Nesta Futurelab, Bristol.

NACCCE (1999) *All Our Futures: Creativity, Culture and Education*. DCMS/DfEE, London.

Papert, S. (1980) *Mindstorms: Children, Computers, and Powerful Ideas*. Harvester, Brighton.

Papert, S. (1993) *Mindstorms: Children, Computers, and Powerful Ideas*. Basic Books, New York; Perseus, Cambridge, MA.

Passey, D., Rogers, C., Machell, J., McHugh, G., Allaway, D. (2003) *The Motivational Effect of ICT on Pupils: Emerging Findings*. DfES, London.

Pittinsky, M. (2002) *The Wired Tower: Perspectives on the Impact of the Internet on Higher Education*. Financial Times/Prentice Hall, Upper Saddle River, NJ.

Ridgeway, J. and McCusker, S. (2004) *Literature Review of E-assessment*. Nesta Futurelab, Bristol.

Wheeler, S. (ed) (2005) *Transforming Primary ICT*. Learning Matters, Exeter.

Wragg, T. (2005) 'The safe road to stagnation' in *Times Educational Supplement*.

CHAPTER 7

Action planning to identify and overcome barriers

Introduction and approaches

So far, this book has aimed to be optimistic and forward-looking in helping teachers, managers and schools identify and overcome the barriers to successful teaching and learning using ICT. The rationale was to tackle each of the areas in which problems might occur:

- procurement
- technical issues
- training
- learning content
- pedagogy.

This rationale was built on the idea that although there is some crossover between these areas, there are some specific issues in each one. In addition, it is hoped that teachers will find it easier to identify the issues if they begin to think about their nature and how they will be categorised.

For some of those who are using this book, some chapters will be more useful than others. For example, trainee teachers may find the sections on content and pedagogy more directly relevant, whereas school managers may find that the chapter on procurement is relevant. Serving teachers will probably find that there is something in each chapter which seems relevant.

Considering these different audiences, writing about action planning is problematic. Each audience and each individual situation will require a different approach. If the solution to making the most of ICT in teaching and learning was easy, someone would have surely found it by now! In fact, the combination of factors influencing ICT in teaching and learning is extremely complex, with factors depending on one another and factors which are outside the scope of ICT. The premise of this book is, however, that recognising and untangling these factors will help teachers and mangers overcome the barriers to teaching and learning using ICT. To this end, action planning is split into three areas:

- Action planning to identify and overcome procurement and technical barriers.
- Action planning to identify and overcome barriers to effective training and professional development.
- Action planning to identify and overcome barriers to effective teaching and learning.

In many schools, these areas may be the responsibility of different people, with school managers in charge of technical and procurement issues, ICT heads of department or subject leaders in charge of training and professional development in ICT, and teachers and those with teaching and learning responsibility being in charge of matters concerned with the curriculum and teaching and learning. In smaller schools, especially in the primary sector, it may be that the responsibility for more than one of these areas falls on the same person. What follows are suggestions which might help teachers, managers and schools identify and overcome the barriers to ICT in their own learning environments.

Action planning to identify and overcome procurement and technical barriers

There are many users of technology who make full use of the potential of the computers and other devices they own. Most personal computers are capable of word and image processing, making video, storing and recording music, storing and sorting data, playing games, connecting to the Internet, sending and receiving email, playing games and much more. How many users really use all these applications fully? The same applies to the multiple functions of mobile phones, portable computers and even games consoles. This raises the question, Are we getting full value out of the technology we already own? This is the first question which should be asked when school managers are reviewing ICT provision. Substantial amounts of money are spent every year in schools on new ICT equipment, but there is rarely any consideration of how much use is being made of the full potential of the existing technology. Only once this is assessed should plans be made for future purchasing.

Another important consideration when buying technology is its fitness for purpose. This means fitness for teaching and learning purposes and for the space available for it: fitness to be used by the teachers who will teach with it, given their levels of expertise; and fitness to be used with the other available technology successfully. In short, technology should be well matched to the setting in which it is going to be used.

The final important issue in action planning to identify and overcome procurement and technical barriers is the issue of funding. Although there are substantial funds available to schools, many of them are 'ring-fenced' or specific to a particular ICT use, for instance interactive whiteboards. This issue is discussed more fully in Chapter 2.

These are the three questions which managers and teachers should investigate when they begin to action plan:

1 What technology do we have at the moment? Are we using it to its full potential?

2 Will investment in new technology fit with the school, the building and the teachers who will use it?

3 Given the restriction on funding, how can we use the money available strategically?

Different situations will require different approaches to these questions, but the following are some suggestions for actions which should help establish the answers to these questions:

● Keep a detailed record of all ICT equipment, including its age and where it is kept.

● Carry out a survey, over a week or two, to gauge how much each piece of equipment is used – this might be done simply by attaching a log sheet to each piece of equipment. One log should be sufficient for a suite of computers.

● Keep an open mind about the use of space in schools. Paper resources can take up a lot of space and some are not often used. Review storage and 'declutter' whenever possible.

● Survey ICT user confidence levels – see below.

● Plan for expenditure several years in advance, taking into account different funding schemes. Although funding plans are always subject to change, plans can usually be altered to take these changes into account.

● Have a 'vision' or 'mission statement' for ICT in teaching and learning. This should help focus planning.

Advice and support

Schools, teachers and managers receive support through LEAs where appropriate, and other bodies in financial planning. There are also some sources of information on the Internet which schools might find useful.

One of the important things to do in action planning is to have a vision of ICT in teaching and learning. This vision should be aspirational. One good source of ideas and motivations is the Nesta Futurelab website. The reports and literature reviews help teachers and managers keep up with future ICT developments and research into educational ICT: http://www.nestafuturelab.org/.

It is also important for schools to make sure they are making the most of what is available. The DfES website contains information about initiatives and is linked to sites which deal with individual initiative such as the laptops for teachers scheme: http://www.lft.ngfl.gov.uk/.

Action planning to identify and overcome barriers to effective training and professional development

Appropriate support and training for teachers is essential for successful ICT in teaching and learning. Unfortunately, although this seems a rather obvious requirement, many teachers' experiences of professional development in this area are inadequate. Often, the problem has been caused by poorly focused training, which has failed to meet the needs of teachers, and by teachers' workloads preventing them from following up what they have learned and turning it into meaningful and useful classroom practice. The Hands on Support Initiative (DfES 2004b; DfES 2004c), as discussed in Chapter 4, seeks to provide training and professional development for teachers which is well matched to their needs.

The processes involved in successful training and professional development for each school, department or individual vary enormously. Therefore it is very important for training providers to establish the needs for those concerned before planning their training.

In the past, some problems in training and professional development were caused by technical issues, such as the hardware and software being unavailable at the time of training. In addition, schools must consider the timing of training carefully. Advances in ICT provision in schools, including training and professional development, must be part of a whole-school programme of development and work in harmony with the other issues on teachers' agendas, such as development of the curriculum, in line with strategies and policies. For this reason those responsible for organising professional development and training must make sure it is part of a whole programme of ICT development rather than an aim in itself.

Finally, teachers must have the time and support to integrate the developments into their practice. Teachers need time and flexibility to experiment with new approaches to teaching and learning with ICT in order to successfully make them a part of their practice.

Therefore, there are three stages which ICT subject leaders or school managers must take into account when planning a programme of training and development:

1   Find out which technical skills and pedagogical approaches each teacher wants to make a priority for his or her professional development.

2   Considering the ICT and school development plan, what is the best approach to the timing of training opportunities?

3   Make sure teachers have the extra time they need to change and develop their professional practice.

Where school managers and ICT subject leaders are able to take these issues into consideration, training stands a good chance of being successful.

Assessing ICT confidence and competence

This first crucial stage of planning ICT training and development needs to be looked at in terms of technical issues and pedagogical approaches. Although one may very well depend on the other, appropriate methods of training may differ. Therefore, finding out about technical training needs separately from the needs of pedagogical professional development should help training to be successful. The following are examples of formats which could be used to ascertain levels of confidence and competence. These are examples only, which can be adapted to meet the needs of specific situations.

Technical confidence questionnaire

Rate your confidence in each aspect on a 3-point scale, with 1 being not at all confident, 2 fairly confident and 3 very confident. These should reflect how confident you feel in doing these things without help in your normal teaching situation.

Table 7.1 Technical confidence questionnaire

Equipment and Peripherals		
1	Use an interactive whiteboard to show a presentation.	
2	Help pupils get out and log on to the wireless network. Troubleshoot where necessary.	
3	Support pupils in the use of a digital camera, including downloading images from the camera.	
Presentation software		
4	Create a teaching presentation using words.	
5	Insert pictures into documents and presentations.	
6	Add presentations to shared areas on the school intranet/VLE.	
The school VLE		
7	Log on to and read messages in the school VLE.	
8	Add files to the school VLE.	
9	Create discussion boards on the school VLE.	
10	Trouble-shoot while pupils use the VLE.	

Confidence and relevance questionnaire

Rate these activities in two ways: first how confident you feel about doing them, and second how much of a priority they are considering your approach to teaching and learning.

Rate your confidence in each aspect on a 3-point scale, with 1 being not at all confident, 2 fairly confident and 3 very confident. These should reflect how confident you feel in doing these things without help in your normal teaching situation.

Rate each in terms of priority, with 1 next to the aspect you think would have the most positive impact on your teaching and learning and 10 as the thing which is a low priority.

Support and advice is available via the Internet to support those planning training and professional development. The Hands on Support initiative, outlined in Chapter 4, should help schools plan appropriate and meaningful support. Downloadable versions of the documents are available at the DfES publications website on Teachernet: http://publications.teachernet.gov.uk/default.aspx?pagemode=publications&ResetBrowse=yes.

Table 7.2 Confidence and relevance questionnaire

		Confidence	Priority
Presentations			
1	Use an interactive whiteboard presentation to support you in explaining a new complex concept, using words, pictures and sounds where appropriate.		
2	Use an interactive whiteboard presentation to encourage pupil participation and engagement in a lesson.		
3	Use a presentation created during the lesson in a plenary.		
Multimedia			
4	Identify areas in your subject where images (still or moving) might support learning.		
5	Organise pupils in using a digital camera in a group of five. Ensure each pupil has a role in the capture and download of images.		
Virtual learning			
6	Identify a range of websites which are relevant and useful to your teaching.		
7	Create links to websites in the VLE.		
8	Start and maintain a discussion using the VLE's discussion board.		
9	Email groups and individuals using the VLE.		
10	Construct and manage learning objects on the VLE.		

In addition, there are a range of reports and support material on the Teachernet ICT site. These can be used in professional development for planning and to inspire debate among teachers: http://www.teachernet.gov.uk/wholeschool/ictis/.

Action planning to identify and overcome barriers to effective teaching and learning

Teaching and learning in schools is undergoing constant change and development. Working under pressure from initiatives and strategies is a way of life for today's teachers. Under this constant pressure, many teachers find it difficult to keep up with everything. Developing teaching and learning with ICT is an aspect of pedagogical development which is embedded in most strategies and initiatives, and is part of this pressure. The question is, How can teachers identify which aspects of the many initiatives can have a positive influence on teaching and learning?

The following are examples of questions which can be used in staff professional development sessions to inspire debate and encourage teachers to examine their own practice. The responses can be used to structure a school's approach to identifying and overcoming barriers to effective teaching and learning using ICT.

- What are the current successful uses of ICT in teaching and learning? Could these be used in other contexts?
- Considering the current curriculum and schemes of work, is ICT use appropriately distributed throughout subjects, phases and areas?
- What use is being made of available ICT support materials?
- How can ICT support pupils of differing abilities?
- In what ways does ICT support pupils in approaching their learning creatively?
- Can ICT help pupils develop their thinking skills?
- What are the best ways to harness the motivational power of ICT for teachers and learners?
- What are the short-, medium- and long-term changes we can make to the curriculum to enable more effective use of ICT?

Developing pedagogy is always challenging because it requires experimentation and investigation into new ideas. There are a number of websites, however, which can support schools and teachers in innovation. For simple ideas and links to new resources, the Teacher Resource Exchange is an excellent resource from lesson plans to videos and websites. Each has been reviewed by teaching professionals. Teachers can sort the available resources by subject, topic, age range and type of lesson: http://www.teachernet.gov.uk/wholeschool/ictis/.

Ultralab is connected to Anglia Ruskin University and specialises in challenging and interesting research into teaching and learning using ICT. The website provides links to their projects. In addition members of the team use blogs to record their ideas and these are useful for keeping up with recent developments in ICT: http://ww3.ultralab.net/.

Action planning formats

Action planning to identify and overcome the barriers to effective teaching and learning using ICT needs to take account of the three areas:

- Action planning to identify and overcome procurement and technical barriers.
- Action planning to identify and overcome barriers to effective training and professional development.
- Action planning to identify and overcome barriers to effective teaching and learning.

It may be that although different members of the school team consider these issues at different times, each area is dependent on the other two. One way to view ICT action planning is to take this three-pronged approach. The following format can help the team bring this approach together:

References

DfES (2004b) *Hands on Support. Guidance and Support for HOS Providers. Secondary.* DfES, London.

DfES (2004c) *Hands on Support. Guidance and Support for HOS Providers. Primary.* DfES, London.

Table 7.3 Action planning format

	Aim	Action	Resources	People	Timescale	Success criteria	Follow-up
Procurement and technical issues							
Training and professional development issues							
Teaching and learning issues							

CHAPTER 8

Conclusions: a brighter future for learning technology – The digital generation

Children growing up in the early twenty-first century are part of a digital culture which was unimaginable even when their parents were their age. From television to music, from games to communications, at home, in shops, in the cinema, almost everywhere children go, they encounter devices which use microchips. This is a challenge to the world of education. How can we make schools a relevant part of the lives of the digital generation?

The only certain thing about the future of ICT in teaching and learning is that it is uncertain. Large-scale funding may depend on political events, and developments in pedagogical approaches and the curriculum may influence the role which ICT plays. Available technology itself changes rapidly, as does the uses to which it is put. Yet while politics, money and educational trends change, one thing remains constant – children come to school to learn. As teachers, school leaders and educationalists it is crucial we remain focused on the best interests of our pupils, the children in the schools of today and tomorrow.

Technology provides some amazing opportunities for learning. It also has the potential to become a hindrance to good teaching and learning. To make the best of the future, the children and their learning must be at the heart of the decision-making progress. For children growing up in early years of the twenty-first century, technology offers a range of opportunities. It also has a range of challenges. It is by balancing these two elements that teachers will guide their schools towards effective use of ICT in teaching and learning. As a conclusion to this book, the opportunities and challenges are examined from the perspective not of the teachers but of the children they teach.

The role of ICT in children's lives

There have been a number of studies into how, when and where children encounter ICT (Hayward, Alty, *et al.* 2003; Kent and Facer 2004). These analyse children's experiences of ICT in respect of a range of factors:

- where children use ICT;
- what they use ICT for;
- how children's age and gender effects their computer ICT;
- what impact the social and economic background of children has on their use of ICT.

Children use ICT in a number of places: home and school as well as places like libraries. Recent developments mean they also use mobile ICT devices (Hayward, Alty, *et al.* 2003). There are few places where ICT can't be accessed to communicate, to research and to play games. The report puts the figure for ICT use among children at 98 per cent. It seems those who do not use ICT in their lives are in a very small minority.

The report goes on to detail where this use takes place:

> 92 per cent of children used computers at school and 75 per cent used them at home.
>
> 49 per cent of young people used computers in a location other than at home or at school.
>
> 22 per cent of 5–18-year-olds used computers at school but not at home.
>
> (Hayward, Alty, *et al.* 2003)

From these statistics, the importance of school ICT is clear – more children encounter ICT at school than at home or in other places. Given that children spend a surprisingly small percentage of their time at school (six hours a day for 37 weeks of the year – works out at about 13 per cent of a school age child's life), it seems that schools are packing plenty of opportunities for ICT into the time that children spend there.

There are some significant differences between what children use ICT for at home and schools. Detailed analysis of a cohort of over 1,800 children living in the South West of England (Kent and Facer 2004) shows that children spend their computer time:

- having fun;
- playing games;
- writing;
- 'fiddling' (playing with the computer);
- emailing;
- using the Internet to get information;
- drawing and making images;
- watching TV and listening to the radio;
- making and designing things;

- downloading software;
- using the web for revision;
- using educational software;
- downloading music;
- organising information;
- watching DVDs;
- composing music;
- making charts and graphs;
- <making or watching films and animations;
- making websites;
- shopping on the web.

The young people were surveyed as to which of these activities they did on a frequent (at least weekly basis) at home and at school. Over 50 per cent used the web for fun and information, wrote and 'fiddled' on the computer at both home and school at least weekly. Games were also a weekly activity at home for 80 per cent and at school for 45 per cent of young people surveyed.

Looking at the range and frequency of ICT activities which young people engage in, it is clear that ICT is an important tool for fun, for learning, for creative activity and for communication.

Opportunities

Given this situation, there is a significant opportunity for schools to make learning in ICT relevant to young people's lives. If children and young people are choosing to make the Internet, games, video, music and other digital activities part of their leisure time, these ought to be part of what they do at school. Surveys of children's attitudes to ICT show a clear motivational benefit from using ICT in teaching and learning and that the use of technology is deeply embedded in young people's culture (Somekh, Lewin, *et al.* 2002). Schools need to harness this motivation and make learning relevant to pupils by reflecting pupils' interests in their teaching methods. However, making 'token' gestures in using ICT in teaching and learning is not sufficient. ICT should be meaningfully embedded in the curriculum and in teaching methods.

Challenges

With the opportunities to motivate pupils and make learning relevant by using ICT in teaching and learning, come challenges. The largely unregulated and rapid growth of the Internet has meant that this resource has a 'dark side'. In early 2004, a survey of over 1,500 9–19-year-olds was undertaken to find out about their use of the Internet (Livingstone and Bober 2004). The survey found that many children have engaged in activities on the web which would be considered as potentially harmful: 57 per cent have seen pornographic images (although most images of this nature are viewed unintentionally), 46 per cent have given out personal information on the Internet and 8 per cent say they have met face-to-face someone they first got to know on the Internet. The report also highlights the fact that parents underestimate the risks their children take online. However, this should not dissuade schools, or parents from allowing children to use the Internet. Part of the job of schools, with parents, is to teach children to use the Internet safely. The issues are summarised in a BECTA publication: http://www.becta.org.uk/corporate/publications/documents/Technology_safely.pdf

Where schools and parents encourage children to use the Internet and technology responsibly and within boundaries set, problems should be minimised.

ICT and learning

> …the nation of the child computer user has been used by state and commercial interests to rehearse, clarify and promote a range of societal, economic and political concerns over the role of new technologies in society.
>
> (Selwyn 2003)

This paper examines the relationship between children's use of computers and the way government and commerce develop ICT. It argues that there are various ways in which the media constructs a relationship between children and computers: children as natural users of computers; children as successful users of computers; children who use computers like adults and children at risk from using computers. The paper sees commerce and government as using these constructs to lead developments in ICT, in short, that computer use in society is governed by the needs of children not adults. This raises some interesting questions: Is ICT seen as something for the younger members of society? If the answer is 'yes', then a second question is raised: Does this mean that ICT and learning *should* be linked closely in schools?

Studies into learning and ICT have begun to explore how technology can impact on knowledge, skills and understanding. These have been focused on a number of areas, including 'creativity' (Loveless 2002). Research such as that cited in this report closely allies ICT development with pedagogical and curricular development. With continuing investment in ICT in schools, it seems likely that ICT and teaching and learning will be increasingly closely linked in the future.

This offers a range of opportunities to support better teaching and learning practices in schools, to provide opportunities for more creative and more individual programmes of learning which better prepare children for their futures socially, professionally and educationally. It also offers some challenges in that ICT can also be used to limit teaching and learning within technological barriers.

Opportunities

The possibilities of computer gaming as an educational tool have been explored in Chapter 6. The massive popularity of computer games in a range of formats, on consoles, on home computers and on mobile devices is a significant phenomenon of young peoples' culture. In the Nesta Futurelab report on this subject, this close relationship is recognised and seen as an opportunity. The review acknowledges that playing computer games can encourage:

- strategic thinking;
- planning;
- communication;
- application of numbers;
- negotiating skills;
- group decision-making;
- data-handling.

(Kirriemuir and McFarlane 2004)

The report calls for teachers to consider how games might be used in schools. Although, it acknowledges, there are a range of 'edutainment' games available, the report examines the shortcomings of these in terms of their limited interest for learners and the scope of what they accomplish when compared with games which are designed for the leisure market.

The future of learning through games lies in building on the successes of the existing games market, and a recognition of the learning opportunities these offer. If education can harness some of the power of the best computer games, there are some significant possibilities.

Challenges

In a recent trial of computer-aided assessment for key stage 3 pupils, one pupil commented that being tested by computer, and having his performance in the test assessed by computer was 'a bit worrying'. He went on to say that he felt 'like computers were taking over the world' (Harrison 2005). While the article reflects many positive responses of pupils to online testing, saying they were more fun, interesting and easier to understand than paper-based tests, the concern of the pupil at computers 'taking over' is a valid one. It is an exaggeration to say that computers could turn our lives into something reminiscent of the experiences of the anti-hero Winston in George Orwell's novel *1984*. However many people, a significant number of them teachers and educationalists, foster a scepticism about the benefits of ICT in education. Teaching and learning, at its fundamental level, is a human activity, based on the relationships between teachers and learners. It seems right to be sceptical that a machine, however sophisticated, could even begin to replicate this complex human interaction. This is not to say that ICT cannot support, and in some cases even improve that interaction, but it cannot replace it.

We must ensure, therefore, that what stimulates development in ICT is not what the technology can do, but what we want the technology to do for us. We must have good teaching and learning constantly in our sight, and consider how ICT can support that. This should ensure that the Orwellian nightmare of a society which is controlled by technology never takes place in our schools, or elsewhere for that matter.

The future of ICT in schools: A hopeful vision

Teaching is often such a challenging business that sometimes it is difficult for teachers in the classroom to keep an eye on the 'big picture' of what they are trying to achieve. The same applies to teaching with ICT. The complexities of teaching with ICT, pedagogical and technical, sometimes make it difficult for teachers to keep an eye on the 'big picture' of what they are trying to achieve with ICT.

The aim of this book is to be forward-looking and optimistic, so to round off, here are some general principles which might help teachers keep an eye on what can be achieved through teaching and learning with ICT.

- ICT can help teachers ground learning in children's real-life experiences, through games, through simulations and through using real experiences, stories and pictures.

- ICT can help teachers and learners communicate with one another in new ways, irrespective of location or timescale.

- ICT can help learners work in different ways, and perhaps in ways which suit their style of learning better.

- ICT can help to include teachers and learners fully in the process of learning, irrespective of situations, disabilities and restrictions.

- ICT can make learning more exciting, engaging and interesting for teachers and learners.

In practice, aiming for these goals can seem challenging, but there are things which can be done, in the short and long term, which can help teachers in each phase achieve these goals.

Foundation Stage

Tomorrow...

Foundation stage teachers can aim to use a digital camera with pupils every day in some way. This should encourage children to become familiar with it and where possible children should be able to take photos. A Polaroid camera is a more expensive but equally instant option. Photos might be useful:

- at outdoor play time to help establish rules about play;
- on a walk round the school grounds or local area;
- in the role play area to encourage children to talk about their play;
- to make a book of members of the class to help establish friendships.

In the future...

Plan to buy foundation stage specific hardware and software. Input devices such as rollerball mice or touch screens may help children develop their independent use of the computer. In this way the computer might be included in classroom activities, for example, as an option in a creative development activity or in the role play area which is set up as an office. Portable ICT devices such as tablet PCs and laptops might be more useful in these circumstances than a traditional 'desktop' PC.

Primary

Tomorrow...

Primary school teachers can take half an hour to look at one piece of software they use regularly, for instance, a word processing package or drawing package, and experiment with features they don't usually use. Examples of these might include:

- hyperlinking pages of word processing documents;
- creating tables in word processing documents and using them to sort data in simple ways;

- inserting pictures taken with a camera into Word documents and using them as a basis for writing;
- using a drawing program to develop pictures which have been drawn by hand and scanned;
- on a photo of a face, using the rubber and brush tools to change the face.

Consider how such activities could be used in a curriculum area where ICT is normally not used.

In the future...

Organising the use of ICT equipment in the primary classroom can be a challenge. Although many schools have computer suites, classes often have only one session a week in the suite. This leaves teachers with a difficulty in organising ICT activities which are integrated into the curriculum. Teachers need to plan ways to do this. If there are computers in the classroom, it might be that a teacher sets up a task for the week linked to a topic or book the class is studying. Each day, the teacher should allocate some children to take their turn at the activity that day. Monitoring and recording computer use for each pupil is essential.

Secondary

Tomorrow...

There are a wide range of Internet-based materials available to teachers and some of these are also suitable as revision for pupils working towards key stage 3 SATs or exams. Using the Curriculum Online website, search for freely available resources to use for revision homework or further study.

In the future...

The use of ICT in secondary schools varies depending on the resources available to the department. However planning strategically as a department to share resources and good practice is important. Including ICT in departmental development plans is essential, especially when different members of the department have different types of expertise. It may also be beneficial if the department sends delegates on ICT training, which they then share with their other colleagues.

Post-16

Tomorrow...

Online testing is controversial but has benefits if it is approached as a method of formative assessment. The Hot Potatoes website provides an easy web-based assessment format which is free of charge to the state school sector: http://hotpot.uvic.ca/. Busy teachers could ask pupils to devise their own tests.

In the future...

There is a wide range of ICT hardware and software available to schools. Much of this can be used to enhance a creative approach to learning. Dataloggers in the lab can inspire science experiments, pupils using digital video cameras can make history and geography projects challenging and enjoyable. Future developments in virtual learning should support pupils in developing electronic records of their research and work. At a time where the post-16 phase is undergoing changes, schools should examine the possibilities for ICT to enhance a creative approach to teaching and learning.

The final word

Teaching and learning with ICT is much easier to talk (and write!) about than it is to do. This book was intended to support teachers at all stages in their career who want to develop their use of ICT. Some of those teachers will be pursing this because they have to. Including ICT in teaching and learning is a compulsory aspect of the curriculum. What I hope to have also demonstrated is that ICT is worth the effort because it can improve teaching and learning by making it more exciting, innovative, motivating, thought provoking and challenging. I have tried to put practical advice in the context of policy and research, because teaching and learning with ICT takes place in real schools, with real teachers and pupils. To them, I wish the best of luck with unlocking teaching and learning with ICT, and I hope that this book has helped in identifying and overcoming the barriers which exist.

References

Harrison, A. (2005) *Online Exam Clicks with Students*. BBC, London. 2005.

Hayward, B., Alty, C., Pearson, S., Martin, C. (2003) *Young People and ICT 2002*. BECTA, Coventry.

Kent, N. and Facer, K. (2004) 'Different worlds? A comparison of young people's home and school ICT use.' *Journal of Computer Assisted Learning*, 20, pp. 440–455.

Kirriemuir, J. and McFarlane, A. (2004) *Literature Review in Games and Learning*. Nesta Futurelab, Bristol.

Livingstone, S. and Bober, M. (2004) *UK Children Go Online*. London, LSE.

Loveless, A. (2002) *Literature Review in Creativity, New Technologies and Learning*. Nesta Futurelab, Bristol.

Selwyn, N. (2003) '"Doing IT for the kids": re-examining children, computers and the "information society".' *Media Culture and Society*, 25, pp. 351–378.

Somekh, B., Lewin, C., Mavers, D., Fisher, T., Harrison, C., Haw, K., and Lunzer, E. (2002) *ImpaCT2: Pupils and Teachers Perceptions of ICT in the Home, School and Community*. BECTA, Coventry.

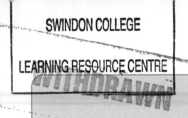
Index

Unlocking Speaking and Listening

Pamela Hodson and Deborah Jones

UNLOCKING SERIES

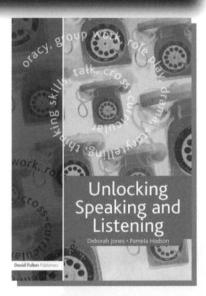

The teaching of Speaking and Listening has again been identified as central to children's learning and literacy development, yet it is an area in which teachers have little confidence. This book aims to address a recognised need by tackling key issues surrounding Speaking and Listening with rigour, depth and a strong focus on research.

The contributors offer practical advice on teaching Speaking and Listening creatively from the Foundation Stage through Key Stages One and Two. It also covers significant inter-related areas:

- Drama and storytelling
- ICT
- English as an Additional Language
- Gifted and talented pupils
- SEN

Written by expert contributors from Brunel University, this book is a vital resource to help both trainee and practising primary teachers understand and promote the importance of Speaking and Listening as an effective tool for learning across the primary curriculum.

Contents: Listening to children's voices: Unlocking speaking and listening in the primary classroom; Fostering speaking and listening in Foundation Stage classrooms; Talking to think: Why children need philosophical discussion; Inclusive approaches to communication with children who have special educational needs; Teachers and children: A classroom community of storytellers; Letting talents shine: Developing oracy with Gifted and Talented pupils; Dynamic talk: Speaking, listening and learning through drama; Speaking and listening: Planning and assessment; Scaffolding learning: Speaking, listening and EAL pupils; Emphasising the "C" in ICT: Speaking, listening and communication.

Pamela Hodson is Principal Lecturer at Kingston University and Deborah Jones is a lecturer in primary English at Brunel University.

£18.00 • Paperback • 198 pages • 1-84312-392-4 • March 2006

David Fulton Publishers Ltd • The Chiswick Centre • 414 Chiswick High Road • London W4 5TF
☎ 0208 996 3610 📠 0208 996 3622 ✉ mail@fultonpublishers.co.uk 🖰 www.fultonpublishers.co.uk
To subscribe to the FREE David Fulton Publishers eNewsletter visit our website and click on 'Newsletter'